Dr. Eddie Ensley is one of the mo[...] Christ that I have ever met. What you learn in this book will bless, comfort, and encourage you. It will deepen your faith, your understanding, and your relationship with your Creator.

RICHARD G. ARNO, PH.D.
Founder, The National Christian Counselors Association
Sarasota, Florida

Deacon Ensley delves so uniquely and thoroughly into our present-day miseries. Then he so tenderly and brilliantly gives the ways, the only real ways, of healing and restoration and new life. Beyond that, Ensley's writing style is warm and comforting—yet firm when it comes to making the necessary changes divine healing requires. What a blessing this book will be!

J. SERVAAS WILLIAMS
Author of Abraham and Sarah *and other historical-biblical novels.*

The Dogmatic Constitution on Divine Revelation (*Dei Verbum*) defined revelation as word plus event and as an invitation to enter into a dialogue with God in the person of Jesus Christ. Deacon Eddie Ensley has provided us with a compelling and inviting spiritual and practical application of this understanding to the life of prayer in which God's word to us and our conversation in return brings the dialogical word of prayer alive in a particular way as an event of transformation and healing in Christ!

MONSIGNOR CHRISTOPHER SCHRECK
Rector/President of Pontifical College Josephinum

Eddie Ensley offers us a profound experience of God's love. His vivid imagery and depth of experience in healing prayer opens us to new and joyful dimensions of intimacy with God and communion with all of Creation. For the many situations we face in our lives, including the grief and confusion we feel when confronted with senseless violence, Ensley expresses his deep empathy and guides us gently into our journey to the heart of God.

BARBARA FLEISCHER
Psychologist, Associate Professor of Pastoral Studies at Loyola University New Orleans.

Deacon Eddie's gentle faith inspires me. I find myself wanting to read the words again slowly, savoring the invitation to awaken our senses so that Christ can heal the hidden, vulnerable places and magnify the places of joy. He has a gift of telling stories where sometimes you will feel surprised, at other times share in grief or pain, and then shift to be lifted up in awe with Our Creator. You will come away echoing the words of his grandfather, "you walk in my soul." As a pastoral counselor, I plan to use many of his guided imageries to lead clients to allow God to heal their broken emotional places. I recommend this book for counselors as a resource, and to individuals who want a rich expansion of the heart.

SUSAN A. SENDELBACH, M.A., D.MIN.
Pastoral Counselor, and Neurotherapist at Anchor Point Counseling Center, Conyers, GA; (former Hospital Chaplain and Campus Minister)

Eddie Ensley invites the reader on a pilgrimage into the depths of oneself—and there to encounter the healing love of God. This journey's challenge is to recognize and affirm the truth that God resides not just in our better or "bright spots," but throughout our entire being. And in this healing adventure we learn to be comfortable with God in the depths of our person where we experience the meaning of personal integrity and the freedom to love.

REV. RICHARD BERG, CSC, PH.D.
Psychologist, dean emeritus College of Arts and Sciences, University of Portland

---

In his books and ministry of over 30 years, Eddie Ensley's message has always been clear: God's love can heal our deepest wounds. In the beautiful guided meditations in *Healing the Soul*, Eddie helps the reader to let go and allow that love to be experienced. This book could not be more timely. With its provocative discussion questions at the end of each chapter, *Healing the Soul* can be a great resource for educators, as well as for individuals in their journey towards healing.

JUDY ESWAY, MA, CT
Author and certified grief counselor

HEALING
THE
Soul

FINDING PEACE
AND CONSOLATION
WHEN LIFE HURTS

Deacon Eddie Ensley, Ph.D.

TWENTY
THIRD *23rd*
PUBLICATIONS
NEW LONDON, CT 06320
WWW.23RDPUBLICATIONS.COM

This book is not intended to offer professional advice or services to the individual reader. The suggestions in this book are not a substitute for visiting a physician, counselor, or psychologist. All matters regarding health require medical supervision. Neither the author nor the publisher shall be liable for any loss or damages resulting from information or suggestions in this book.

The stories from this book that involve people other than the author make use of composites created by the author from his experience with real people in his ministry. Names and details of the stories have been changed, and any similarity between names and stories of individuals in this book to individuals known to readers is purely coincidental.

Twenty-Third Publications
A Division of Bayard
One Montauk Avenue, Suite 200
New London, CT 06320
(860) 437-3012 or (800) 321-0411
www.23rdpublications.com

ISBN: 978-978-1-58595-921-1
Library of Congress Catalog Card Number : 2013945644
Printed in the U.S.A.

DEDICATION

*This book is dedicated to
the memory of my grandparents;*

IRVIN (POP) ALEXANDER ENSLEY
ROSE FRANCES ENSLEY
TINY POPE CRITTENDEN
and WALTER H. CRITTENDEN
As well as to CHARLIE
(CharliePop) HARRIS *and* MARY
HARRIS *who were
like grandparents to me.*

Contents

FOREWORD

*"Clean the inside of cup and dish first so that
the outside may become clean as well."*

<small>JESUS TO THE PHARISEES, MATTHEW 23:26</small>

I have known Eddie Ensley since he was a very young man, and he has always had passion and skill for healing real people with their real sufferings. He knows that those sufferings are first of all and most deeply interior. Until the unconscious is touched, until the world of memories, shame, guilt, handicap, early life conditioning, abuse, and the emotions that follow from all of these are brought into full consciousness and offered to God, nothing external ever changes for long. As the author of Ephesians puts it, "That which is exposed by the light is illuminated, and all that is illuminated will itself turn into light" (5:13–14). That, in a word, is the Christian ministry of healing, and in this book you are being taught by a master who has practiced this healing work for most of his life, along with his faithful co-worker, Deacon Robert Herrmann.

These lovely and loving meditations will illuminate "the inside" of our cups and our dishes, and then the outside will invariably take care of itself. We will know what we need to do and what we now can do "in the light."

Let me invite you to Deacon Eddie's wonderful healing ministry through the words of the 15th-century mystic poet of India, Kabir. He names the mystery of inner healing so well:

> *O 'FRIEND! hope for Him while you live,*
> *know while you live,*
> *understand while you live:*
> *for in life deliverance abides.*
> *If the ropes that bind you are not broken while liv-*
> *ing, what hope of deliverance in death?*
> *It is but an empty dream, that the soul shall have*
> *union with Him because it has passed*
> *from the body:*
> *If He is found now, He is found then,*
> *If not, we do but go to dwell in the City of Death.*
> *If you have union now, you shall have it hereafter.*

This fine book from Eddie Ensley will significantly help you find "Him" now—and waste no more time in any city of death.

Fr. Richard Rohr, O.F.M.

Center for Action and Contemplation
Albuquerque, New Mexico

CHAPTER 1

Healing the hurt places

s I was being introduced, I clung tightly to a quarter in my pocket. Rubbing its rough edges against my fingers seemed to reduce my tension slightly. Like many speakers, I am always a little tense before I speak; I believe they call it preperformance anxiety. This time I felt it keenly.

One of the members of the diocesan renewal committee that had invited us to do the retreat, a young family practice physician named Kate, had greeted me with scarcely veiled skepticism and hostility at supper. "As a physician, as a medical scientist, I have a question for you. Do you really think prayer can bring about emotional healing? Isn't emotional healing accomplished through therapy and medication?"

I put on a calm face, though I didn't feel calm inside. I answered her that I thought therapy and medications played a central role, but opening up to God's love in prayer can also bring us to wholeness. God's touch can change us wonderfully, not only in cases of entrenched sadness or anxiety, but in our everyday emotional lives. I wanted to tell her that scientific studies backed up that truth, but decided that challenging her on her own turf would just confuse things further.

Though I hoped my short answer would help her understand, her words had stung, and I let them throw me off balance.

I was about to give the first session of a weekend retreat designed to lead people into deep inner peace and healing, even though at that moment my own heart was less than peaceful.

As I began the talk, I looked down into the audience and saw Kate's sterile, antiseptic expression that scarcely masked her skepticism and anger. I stumbled through the first few sentences, and then realized I couldn't finish the talk. I moved on to the guided prayer experience, playing a slow version of Bach's "Jesu" on the audio system as soft background to the meditation. As I paused in the stillness, I realized one more time that it was not my words or style or knowledge of theology or psychology that would bring healing, but God's all-feeling compassion and love. We were just providing the spiritual and emotional space for people to open up to that love.

As I began to enter into the quiet myself, my anxiety receded. I felt a loving and warming energy pour over me as if I were in a shower of light. I sensed others entering that shower of light with me. Tears softly coursed down people's faces. A thick, warm, loving calmness came over us, knitting our hearts together. It was as though in the silence we were now breathing one breath and experiencing the reality that one Heart beats in all of us. I gently and slowly continued the meditations, leading the group in remembering past joys and imagining a scene from Scripture.

Toward the end of the prayer experience, I noticed that Kate was sobbing. Hers were not the shallow, tight, frantic sobs that come from hopelessness, but the deep, purifying sobs that come from finally letting loose deeply entrenched pain. After we finished the session, Kate took me aside and told me her story, letting me know what had happened to her during the prayer experience.

She started off telling me that her initial hesitation about healing prayer was not really from scientific skepticism but from her own fear of looking inward.

Her mother had died of cancer when Kate was eight. In his grief, her father had become more and more dependent on Kate, his only child, for emotional nurture; he was asking for an adult emotional support that no child is capable of giving. As his drinking habit developed into alcoholism, he abused her first with violent words and then with violent actions. She showed me a scar on her hand from a cigarette burn and another above her eye from a belt buckle. A crash into a bridge abutment killed her father when she was 11, after which a loving aunt reared her and sent her through school.

The shock, the scars of what had happened to her, bored into the center of her being. Deep inside her heart she blamed herself for her father's death. Her emotions shut down, her personality became rigid. If only she had loved him enough, she had always thought, he wouldn't have turned to alcohol.

She then told me what happened during the prayer experience: "I felt an injection of love warming my heart, warming my body," she said. "When you asked us to remember joyful times, I went back to the time before my mother got sick. I saw the three of us happy, laughing, enjoying homemade ice cream on the back porch. We were happy then. In that memory, for the first time in my adult life, I felt my daddy's love. I know he cared for me, cherished me. He just couldn't handle Mother's death. I felt grief and pain too, grief that he is gone, grief that he didn't recover. The hurt and the grief I felt as we prayed were immense, but the sense of love and caring was even greater."

Kate continued the journey that began during the retreat. She started seeing a Christian psychotherapist so that the healing would continue. She initiated a daily program of healing prayer. When I saw her next, the hostility that had covered shame had been replaced by a gentleness and strength that drew from the wellsprings of her being.

Loved deep within

The majority of caregivers no longer share Kate's initial hesitation about healing prayer. More and more they see spirituality having a vital role in not only emotional but physical healing.

How much useless energy is spent digging for painful memories when the real hunger is for loving affirmation—affirmation that allows the hurt we cannot reach despite all our searching and desire to come to the surface. The deeper levels of our psyches won't let go of the tightly guarded hurt until confronted with love and nurture strong enough to replace the hurt. Then, our inward parts that clutch so tightly to pain begin to trust and let go.

Many of the prayer experiences we use in this book and on our retreats are designed to feed our deeper selves with affirmations of God's love. The prayer experiences instill hope, but not the surface kind of hope that suggests we can avoid reality by thinking "nice" thoughts. The prayer experiences bring hope by filling the inner recesses of our being with the central reality of faith: that we are created by a loving God who sent his Son to redeem us. We are grasped by God's affirmation. We experience his love at the very heart of things—a love that cannot and will not let us go. And that love makes all things fresh and new.

When we open our hearts wide to God's caring, the deeper roots of our nature find the permanent soil of an infinite love. We find in the cellars of our souls an ocean of infinite rest that gives meaning to our seemingly endless activities. There is a place within where the sea is always calm and the boats are steady. Christian healing prayer takes our awareness to that place. The kingdom of God, Jesus said, is within us.

When we enter into this kind of deep prayer, we are taken into the arms of a God who will never forsake us from his embrace. As we surrender ourselves to the power of Another, to something greater than ourselves, a force is mobilized within that helps affirm our goodness and wholeness.

Yet many of us, like Kate, fear this opening to love. We know that as we relax our guard and let love in, we will feel the hurts we spend so much energy trying not to feel, and we fear these feelings will overwhelm us. But like Kate's experience and that of many others I have known show, when our guard relaxes because love has touched us, it goes down at just the right pace.

Our pain didn't come in an instant, and our healing doesn't come in an instant. Real and lasting healing resembles the gentle and gradual changing of seasons rather than an overpowering summer thunderstorm.

We may never discover the origin of some of our pain, and that's okay. We don't always need to know where it came from to let it go. Romans 8:26 tells us that when we do not know how to pray, the Spirit prays through us with sighs too deep for words. Each of us is a fathomless depth and only God can know us fully. In meditation we give the Holy Spirit permission to search those depths. As our healing unfolds, at times we will find that a hurt is welling up inside and we don't know why. When that happens, we can grieve and weep and let go of our grip. This is what I believe Paul meant by sighs too deep for words.

Over a period of time, as prayer deepens the work of healing in our lives, a deep joy will root itself in the wellsprings of our being. The sunshine will appear to have more splendor and we shall be able to feel the warmth of words expressed by others rather than suspect ill will hidden in them. We learn to drink in the beauty of each present moment. The trees, the stars, the hills, the touch of another human being appear to us as symbols aching with a meaning that can never be uttered in words. Nature begins to reflect the eternal. Water does more than wash our limbs; it brightens our hearts. The earth we walk on does more than hold our bodies; it gladdens our minds, transmitting to our being the almost maternal tenderness of God.

St. Bernard of Clairvaux on the curative power of prayer:

"O good Jesus, from what great bitterness have you
not freed me by your coming, time after time? When
distress has made me weep, when untold sobs and

*groans have shaken me, have you not anointed
(me)...with the ointment of your mercy and poured
in the oil of gladness? How often has not prayer
raised me from the brink of despair and made me
feel happy in the hope of pardon? All who have had
these experiences know well that the Lord Jesus is a
physician indeed..."*

PRAYER

Dear Lord, teach me to open up the torn parts of my soul to
your deep redeeming love. Like most people, at times I have
gone through times of pain and loss. Teach me to pray that
quiet prayer in which I take a long, lingering look at your
infinite beauty. May your beauty draw me outside of myself,
so that I may spend and give myself to your world and to your
church in the same way you gave to us all. Amen.

DISCUSSION QUESTIONS

1. Have there been times in your life when prayer eased
   your stress or pain? Tell about such a time.
2. Many of us, like Kate in this story, have losses we have
   not grieved. At some point, the touch of God gave us the
   courage to finally grieve. Has there been such a time in
   your life?
3. What have been some of the times God has touched
   your life with his love? Tell about one of them.

CHAPTER 2

What is healing prayer?

How can I draw close to God? This is a question that all of us ask. At times it throbs like a toothache. At other times it lies buried beneath the clutter of everyday busyness. But the question remains always with us.

We yearn to draw close to God because there have been special grace-filled times in all our lives when the mysterious at-homeness of his love caressed and enveloped us. Such times usually sneak up on us unexpectedly. Perhaps you are running along the beach. You cease to be aware of the movement of your muscles or the splashing of your feet in the sand. The sound of the breaking waves stills and calms your mind. You seem one with the sea, the beach—you feel connected. Your fears leave you for a moment. You do not think of God; you experience him. He seems closer to you than the blood that surges through your veins. From the cellar of your soul you call him Father.

Or perhaps such a close encounter comes as you tenderly touch and reverence the skin of your spouse in the midst of the marriage caress. Maybe it occurs in the unexpected sense of love and peace you feel in the midst of tragedy, when the person you thought would never leave you lies in a cool metal box awaiting burial. Such times come in traditional ways too, while you are reading the Bible, receiving communion, or voicing your praise. These times tantalize us, tease us, and make us hungry for more. They put us in touch with dimensions of our life that are missing—parts of ourselves we knew were there all along but had lost contact with.

This book presents practical pathways to growing close to God and becoming whole—ways so simple and so obvious that we easily overlook them. Learning Christian healing prayer will be the adventure of discovering who you really are and loving who you really are. As you increasingly open your heart to the love of God in prayer, you will more and more learn to love the people around you. A fresh joy will root itself deep in the cellar of your soul. As the new love and life within you help you to spend yourself for God, others, and the poor, you can begin to say with St. Paul, "It is not I who live but Christ who lives within me" (Gal 2:20).

Opening doors

Some things defy easy definition. No one definition or even a thousand definitions come close to describing God or love or hope. We sing, tell stories, and paint pictures with words to get at realities that are larger than life.

So it is with healing prayer. In working on this book I searched for a word-picture, story, or image that would describe it. Although I ran scores of images through the slide projector of my mind, I couldn't find one that by itself would convey the reality of healing prayer. I soon found that a number of different metaphors are needed.

One especially vivid picture description is based on an early memory. My mind returns to the simple white-stucco house my grandparents rented from the cotton mill where they worked. The first thing I saw every time I entered their tiny living room was a faded and sentiment-filled picture of Jesus, staff in hand, knocking on the door of a house. The door was special; it had no outside latch. Under the picture was a written explanation. It said that Jesus stood at the door of our hearts knocking, but that he would not barge in or open the door himself. He was gentle; he respected our freedom. He wanted to be invited in. The latch was on the inside of our hearts. We could decide to let him in. The picture quoted the words of the King James Bible: "Behold, I stand at the door and knock. If any man hear my voice and open up to me, I will come in and sup with him and he with me" (Rev 3:20).

For me this old painting is an apt description of Christian healing prayer. In this prayer we unlatch the doors of our hearts so Christ can fill us with his gospel and his love. And we open the door to him not once but countless times. Our hearts have many doors and many rooms. The art of Christian healing prayer is the art of learning to open those doors to the endless beauty of our Eternal Lover.

Healing prayer is prayer that sinks below the surface of conscious thought. This is much of what is meant by the phrase "praying with our whole hearts." The concept of the subconscious is accepted by almost everyone today. Our minds are often compared to icebergs. Only the smaller part of an iceberg protrudes above the surface. So it is with our consciousness; the larger part, the real us, lies below the surface. Here are stored old memories, good and bad, the fresh, bright, wonderful memories of early childhood, as well as traumas buried so deep we wall them off from everyday awareness. Here resides our sexuality. Here, too, is the buried sublimity of our spirit as well as the cesspool of our darkness. Healing prayer lets prayer sink to these hidden parts.

Scripture speaks of these depths: "For the inward mind and heart of a man are deep!" (Ps 64:6B). "For he knows the secrets of the heart" (Ps 44:21). "The Lord sees not as man sees; man looks on the outwards appearance, but the Lord looks on the heart" (1 Sam 16:7). "The Lord searches all hearts, and understands every plan and thought" (1 Chron 28:9).

Motivational researcher Anne White, in *Healing Adventure*, summed up this need for the transformation of our subconscious:

> *If your faith is grounded in the subconscious mind, it will sustain you through any crisis. If it is no deeper than your conscious mind, it will desert you in the moment you are off guard. Its God-given power is amazing.*

Jesus Christ knew all about the subconscious mind and the

part it played in our lives. Despite the profound interest in meditation our modern culture has developed over the last few decades, we are an outward-turned, extroverted society. We are not at home with inner silence, with our inner selves. That is why many run from solitude as quickly as we run from a mugger. Yet when we open the inner doors to God's unfathomable love, we find healing for our deepest wounds and the release of a whirlwind of strength for creative loving and creative living.

How easy it is for our prayer to stay on the surface. Surface prayer is more like dictation than conversation. It tends to be a one-way monologue. We tell God what we want him to do, ask him to bless our plans, and then go merrily on our way. Saint Catherine of Siena, that feisty, fiery, loving woman of prayer who lived in the fourteenth century, summed up this attitude. She was once asked why God no longer conversed with people in the familiar personal way he did in times past. She answered, "God is no longer as personal as He once was because instead of treating Him as the Master and seeing ourselves as the disciple, we treat Him as the disciple and act like we are the Master."

It is so easy to view God as a heavenly bellhop rather than the tender lover of humankind, in fact all creation, whose touch can mend the cracked parts of our souls.

In short, instead of praying "Speak, Lord, your servant is listening," we pray, "Listen, Lord, your servant is speaking."

The special difference

Meditation and contemplation, on which healing prayer is based, have become popular in our culture over the last couple of decades. Some corporations have even set aside special meditation rooms for their top executives, hoping this will help these executives avoid heart attacks. Meditation is in. It lowers blood pressure, prevents disease, reduces stress, helps your sex life, and improves your golf score—so the talk shows and popular magazines tell us. And they are right. Secular meditation does bring some of these benefits. So does Christian healing prayer.

What, then, makes the Christian approach different?

Love!

That's what makes the difference. The core of Christian healing prayer is love: loving God, loving yourself, loving people, loving the whole world. As Saint Augustine put it, "True, whole prayer is nothing but love."

At its heart Christian healing prayer is not just a great set of benefits. Yes, the benefits are there, but they are secondary. All Christian prayer goes beyond the category of usefulness, beyond an enhanced ability to play a better tennis game or get more out of jogging. It offers nothing less than a fiery and eternal love affair with the passionate and all-compassionate Lover who dances throughout the cosmos and in the bosom of our own hearts. Christianity stands under the shadow of a personal God. We believe in a God who cares, who is active in the world, the Yahweh who weaves his way through the story of ancient Israel, the story of Jesus, and the personal stories of each of us.

Healing prayer is a powerful interchange of love with God in the cellar of our souls. It is as Saint Bonaventure so strikingly put it, "the fire that totally inflames us and carries us into God" till we become "inflamed in the very marrow by the fire of the Holy Spirit." In Christian meditation, we open up the inner passageways of our core being and allow this Passionate

One of Israel, the God of Jesus, to express his love to us.

All prayer begins with God's action toward us. Healing prayer is taking a sunbath in his caring, "an inner bath of love into which the soul plunges itself," as Saint Jean Vianney put it. In healing prayer we do nothing less than allow God to love us.

The whole of us

Christianity is the earthiest religion. It takes this world very seriously. "God so loved the world that he gave his only Son" (John 3:16).

There is no special spiritual section inside us barricaded from the rest of us. God wants to involve each particle of our being, down to the cells of our fingernails, in our love affair with him. So Christian healing prayer involves not just our religious side, but our sexuality, our bodies, our intellects, our relationships with others, our work. All become part of our prayer.

It is not so much that we pray as that we *become* a prayer. An early biographer of Saint Francis, Thomas of Celano, describes how Francis gave his whole self over to God in prayer: "All his attention and affection he directed with his *whole being*...to the Lord, not so much praying as becoming himself a prayer." So it should be with us.

This book will carry you on a journey into God. Some of the themes of the prayer experiences may at first not seem particularly religious. They include personal relationships, the healing of past hurts, and learning how to love. This is because God is concerned with all of us, and when we pray, when we meditate, we present all of ourselves to him.

The journey deeper into God's love hurts. In falling in love with anyone there is pain. We open up the different rooms of our hearts to Christ, and he sweeps them clean, then gets out the mop and scrubs away the encrusted grime. So there are times we must look at the grime and together with God take care of it. This is no lark. Facing the grunge inside of us hurts. Nikos Kazantzakis, in describing this decision to yield to God's cleansing, healing therapy, wrote: "God is fire and you must walk on it...dance on it. At that moment the fire will become cool water. But until you reach that point, what a struggle, my Lord, what agony!"

Loving what God loves

Saint Francis of Assisi once said, years after he had begun his journey of prayer, that the things he formerly despised were now sweet to him and the things he once loved he now disliked.

When you fall in love with someone, your likes begin to change. You begin to love the things that person loves. When we fall in love with God, we first begin to love other Christians. The New Testament says that we know that we have passed from death to life when we begin to love fellow believers. We realize that we are on this journey with others—with friends, with family, with the church.

Healing prayer, unlike some secular forms of meditation, is not a solitary, introspective, belly-gazing experience. We are not saved alone. We are not healed alone. We are saved and healed together with one another and all creation. There is an outward movement in prayer as well as an inward movement. We seek an ongoing involvement with brothers and sisters. We begin to love and serve the poor as Jesus loves and serves the poor. We become deeply involved in living out our love relationship in everyday life—loving God in those around us. We realize that the whole of the cosmos groans, like us, for completion.

Scripture journey

"Behold, I stand at the door and knock; if any one hears my voice and opens the door, I will come in to him and eat with him, and he with me. He who conquers, I will grant him to sit with me on my throne, as I myself conquered and sat down with my Father on his throne" (**Rev 3:20-21**).

Take some time to enter into the ease of deep relaxation. Put on some soothing instrumental music. Allow yourself to enter into a deep calm. We will be inviting Jesus into the depths of our unconscious life, and in doing so we will say a deeper yes to him. If you have difficulty imagining this scene, skip ahead to chapter 5 and then return to this meditation.

You are out in the woods, and in front of you is a hill. On the side you see the entrance to a cave; a door blocks your passage. The cave symbolizes your unconscious, your deep heart. There reside bright gifts, learnings, parts of yourself that are rich and vital and that you have forgotten or that have fallen asleep, gifts that have never been given, a diamond mine of sparkling gems.

Also locked away down there are the children of your pain, as Flora Wuellner, author of *Prayer, Stress, and Our Inner Wounds*, has called them: the children that you once were, the children that were once hurt and "have been buried so deeply down inside that you can't hear their crying anymore." Deep inside you, too, are the healthy children that you once were, alive and vibrant.

As you look at the entrance of the cave, you sense someone walking up behind you. It is Jesus. He places his hand on your shoulder, and you feel the peace that his touch brings. Jesus will be entering this cave and going down into its depths to comfort the hurting children. You are not to go down with him, but you walk to the door and open it for Jesus. As he descends into the depths, you stay outside the cave door, praying for him. Down inside, he is embracing the wounded children in long, lingering, tender embraces; cradling them; comforting them; enfolding them in a total love, a pure love. He wipes away their tears.

After a long time, you hear Jesus coming back up. When he opens the door, an immense, radiant light pours from the cave. In his hand is a beautiful diamond that sparkles with intense brightness. You immediately sense the meaning of this diamond. It is a part of you that has been there all along, hidden away from your consciousness. Jesus walks toward you and presses it into your hand with the palm of his hand. You feel the healing flow up through your arm. As you clutch it tightly, an incredible power rushes through your body. As the diamond merges with your hand, a vast brightness fills your whole body. Somehow you know that in the upcoming days and weeks you will discover the significance of this gift in the midst of your daily living. A new talent, a new ability to love, a new enthusiasm may begin to burst forth in you.

Jesus goes back down again. You can hear the sounds of laughter and joy and fun from inside the cave. Jesus is playing with the children you once were. They are healthy, vibrant children. He also plays with the children that he comforted who are on their way to being healed. After a while, you hear him coming up. He walks out the door, bringing with him one of the healthy children, one of the children who is spontaneous and loves fun. What is your reaction on seeing that child, that child that you once were?

Jesus introduces the happy child to the adult you. Play with that child for a while. How does it feel to play? Just enjoy yourself. When you are finished, take the child in your arms. You will find that the child merges with you, flowing into you. Joyousness and wonder flow throughout your body. You suspect that in the next few days you'll be looking out on this world with a fresh, childlike wonder; a new playfulness, a new lightness, a new ease will come into your life.

*THE FIRST PART OF THIS MEDITATION IS ADAPTED FROM
PRAYER, STRESS, AND OUR INNER WOUNDS, FLORA S. WUELLNER
(NASHVILLE: UPPER ROOM, 1985).

DISCUSSION QUESTIONS

1. While Jesus was in the cave with the hurt children of your past, comforting them, what went through your mind?
2. What do you think it means for your "whole being" to become a prayer? What part has prayer played in your own personal unfolding as a person?
3. What do you think the phrase "We are not saved alone" means?

CHAPTER 3

The Jesus Prayer:

A pathway into the deep calm of God

Anna, an old friend of mine, had just lost her social work job. Because of busyness, she forgot to file a required report—a grave error—and her agency terminated her. House and car payments had to be made. Her daughter had just started college and needed help with tuition. For three or four weeks after she lost her job, the stress weighed heavily on Anna. Her mind constantly turned over the possible dire outcomes. Without an income, she could lose her house and car in two months.

She wanted to talk her worries over with God, but worry clouded her mind and she couldn't get the conversation going. However, she had recently read about the Jesus Prayer, an ancient Catholic and Orthodox way of praying, and decided to try it out.

She settled into her chair and began repeating "Jesus, Lord Jesus." At first she was too conflicted even to cry. But after softly repeating the Jesus Prayer for 30 minutes, the weight of her burden seemed to lessen. Serenity began to take over, and gentle tears of relief coursed down her face. As the Jesus Prayer warmed and calmed her heart, she began conversing with God again.

While prayer may not always solve every problem, it can calm the storms inside us so it becomes easier to make prudential decisions. Such was the case with Anna. She prayed the Jesus Prayer regularly, along with Scripture reading and conversational prayer, and these disciplines strengthened her resolve to tackle the issues she faced. She talked with local contacts about other job possibilities. She called different agencies and local colleges. Finally, she landed a job as an instructor teaching social work at a nearby college and added to that some part-time work at a private agency. She made enough to make the house and car payments, plus help with her daughter's college tuition.

Through the centuries, Christians in the midst of stress have turned to prayers such as the Jesus Prayer to ease them into stillness. Over the years the Jesus Prayer has generally crystallized into the phrase "Lord Jesus Christ, Son of God, have mercy on me, a sinner." The exact wording is not as important as the intention behind it. Orthodox Christians, who have a long history of praying the Jesus Prayer, use a variety of forms. Eastern Christians view any invocation of the Holy Name of Jesus as an authentic Jesus Prayer.

The Jesus Prayer and similar prayers are not recited simply

as a means to attain stress relief. Rather, the prayer invites God into the far reaches of the soul. What calms us, stills us, and gives us rest is his presence within.

How to pray the Jesus Prayer

You can pray the prayer anytime and in any circumstance: while falling asleep, waiting in the grocery line, taking a walk, or riding in a car. Even though you can pray anywhere and anytime, be sure to take 15 to 20 minutes of quiet time to pray the Jesus Prayer each day so the prayer can tenderly warm the interior parts of your heart. Most people offer the Prayer while seated. Find a chair that is not too hard: otherwise, you will fidget with discomfort. Use a chair that is comfortable but at the same time supports your back in an upright position.

Start by surrendering to God

Begin your time of prayer by first abandoning yourself and your prayer time into God's care. Ask him to take charge. Perhaps say: "Lord, I turn this prayer time over to you. Do with me what you will." Others prefer the Scriptural prayer: "Father, into your hands I commend my spirit" (Lk 23:46). After you have surrendered your prayer time into God's hands, begin softly saying your Jesus Prayer. Say it out loud, if possible, or at least under your breath.

When your thoughts wander

We all have busy attics. Wandering thoughts are part of being human. I'm sure Jesus had wandering thoughts when he prayed; he was human, after all. Wandering thoughts in prayer are not sinful; they are natural. You didn't will to have these thoughts; they came unbidden. Wandering thoughts in prayer can be a symptom of pent-up stress; the thoughts were with us all along, suppressed, pushed down, and locked inside.

Think of what happens when a capped bottle of cola is shaken. The bottled-up fizz creates great pressure inside the bottle. Finally, when the cap is taken off, the fizz spews out the top, relieving the pressure.

Our busyness and preoccupations cap the thoughts within us. When we take time to say the Jesus Prayer we take the cap off, and the thoughts, which were with us all along but hidden, emerge into our consciousness.

Gently turn your thoughts back to prayer. Don't add to your stress by becoming angry with yourself. After all, the last act of your will before a random thought emerged was an act of loving God, saying the Jesus Prayer. You didn't suddenly say, "I'll interrupt my prayer and choose to have a wandering thought instead." Remember, you surrendered yourself to God for the length of your prayer time. What happens in that prayer time is God's business. When a wandering thought interrupts, the best way to handle it is simply to notice it, then let it pass by. Then, return to saying your Jesus Prayer. Think of a wandering thought as a bird that flies by in the air; you notice it and let it fly away, but you don't make a nest for it. Father William Meninger, a Trappist monk, tells us, "If in the course of a thirty-minute prayer time, wandering thoughts interrupt your prayer a hundred times and you return to saying your prayer each time, you have made a hundred separate acts of loving God."

Lovingly rest in God
After you finish saying your Jesus Prayer, rest in the love of

God. More than anything else God simply wants to love us. And as Saint Augustine said, "He loves every one of us as if we were the only ones he had to love." Let your heart sink into the ease of silent adoration.

A Prayer to the Holy Name

Dear Lord, may your holy name ever be on our tongues, warm our hearts, and quiet our minds. For the name Jesus holds more power than the entire universe. In your name is comfort, consolation, peace, and stillness. The name of Jesus calms our storms, smooths our pathways, brightens our lives, and stills our hearts.

Discussion Questions

1. Talk about a time when a burden you were carrying inside lightened because of prayer.
2. What do you think it means to "lovingly rest in God"?
3. Has there ever been a time when prayer has so calmed you it was easier to make prudential decisions? Tell about that time.
4. What do you think it means to say that prayer can brighten our lives?

CHAPTER 4

How imagination prayer heals

J ust after I finished a talk on God's peace at a Midwest mission, Jane, a middle-aged woman, approached me. "I worry so much," she said. Immediately, her worries poured out of her mouth in a torrent. Obviously she needed more than the two or three minutes I had available to talk with her right then. I suggested that we meet in a church office the next day. When we met, I soon found that Jane worked full time at nights, while attending school in the day to earn her nursing degree. She made a C on a mid-term and feared failing. Her worries so distracted her, she feared losing her job. She spoke of even more imaginary "scenarios of doom."

As I listened to her, I thought imagination prayer could help her. I wanted her to turn her active imagination from harmful scenes to positive ones. I pulled out the Bible and prayerfully read the 23rd Psalm to her to help her calm down. Then I read the story of Jesus calming the storm. I said to her, "Imagine the scene of Jesus quieting the storm. Imagine yourself in the boat with Jesus and the disciples. Huge waves toss the boat around. Rain pounds down on you. The wind howls. The disciples wake Jesus and he says, 'Peace, be still.' Then the storm ceases, replaced by calm. Picture Jesus coming to you in the boat, taking your hand. His love and peace fill you, and your stress begins to leave you.

"Now Jesus whispers, 'Peace. Be still,' just to you."

I asked her to rest a while in the stillness. After we closed, her face looked serene and drained of stress. She looked at me, and then said, "When Jesus said, 'Peace, be still,' my worries greatly lessened." I reminded her that imaginative prayer doesn't eliminate the reality of life's stresses, but it can give us a greater ability to manage those stresses. We can use our imagination to conjure up distressful scenes, or we can use it to center on God and God's peace. Jane still needed to face her problems. Now, however, she possessed another prayer tool to carry her into the loving welcome of God's arms.

Is imaginative prayer scriptural?

The word *meditate* frightens some Christians. They think of fake gurus in robes coming from the east beating drums and selling peace at a price. Let's not let this popular but mistaken idea stop us from meditating. Meditation is an ancient Christian practice found and written about in both the Protestant and Catholic traditions alike. It is not something imported into Christianity. You can find imagination prayer in the Bible and throughout all the Christian centuries. In Christian meditation we don't blank our minds or try by our own wills to achieve some exalted state. Instead, we center our hearts on God. Guided meditation is really a form of prayer leading to contemplative stillness. Some of the psalms are imaginative meditations, especially Psalm 23. The words carry anyone who prays it into green pastures and still waters and leads them through the valley of the shadow of death where "Thou art with me."

Early Christians used imaginative meditation. In the fourth century, Cyril of Jerusalem used guided imagery in the lectures he used to prepare people to enter the church. Scribes recorded the lectures, and scholars preserved them to this day.

In the Protestant and Orthodox traditions, guided meditations are found primarily in hymns such as the beloved gospel hymn "In the Garden." Through these meditations we discipline the imagination, causing it to dwell on eternal themes rather than present circumstances, real or illusory. In this way, God is able to break in and offer comfort and consolation at our weakest and most fearful moments.

Why a picture is worth a thousand words

Imagination is the language of the unconscious. Before we could think and speak, we thought in images. At nighttime we dream in images. Often athletes use visualization to picture themselves performing well, and they find that their imagination enhances their performance. For the most part, our imagination is undisciplined. We fall prey to images we receive from our culture and especially through the media. Edward Hallowell, a Christian psychiatrist who teaches at Harvard Medical School, calls constant worry "a disease of the imagination." He writes, "The imagination is a two-edged sword...you can use it to dream of good stuff, or you can use it to dream up bad stuff."

In Christian meditation, we discipline the imagination and use it to open ourselves to the God of Scripture. Pictures go straight to the heart in a way words never can. That is why Jesus told stories. He gave people verbal pictures to reach the inmost places of their souls.

In the Sermon on the Mount, Jesus said, "Look at the birds of the air; they neither sow nor reap nor gather into barns, and yet your heavenly Father feeds them" (Mt 6:26). Jesus painted pictures with words, like the stained-glass windows that adorn the majority of Christian churches. Mental images of biblical scenes are like painted prayers. Saint Ignatius Loyola took this a step farther by encouraging people to pray by putting themselves in gospel scenes. You may say, "Well, I don't have much of an imagination." That's OK. Just having a sense of a scene suffices.

How to let God penetrate your imagination

One way to use your imagination in prayer is to pick a scene from the gospels, preferably one that includes Jesus. Before you begin this prayer exercise, prepare yourself by sitting in a comfortable chair and relaxing.

There are many ways to relax, to put yourself in a frame of mind to be able to enter fully into meditation. Some people use the Jesus Prayer, for instance, as a way of letting God calm them.

Imagining themselves in a favorite place such as the seashore calms others.

Do what you need to do to get ready. Breathe deeply...relax.

Now imagine the scene from the gospel you have chosen. Place yourself in the scene.

A GUIDED MEDITATION: SITTING WITH JESUS

Close your eyes. Imagine another chair beside you.

In your mind's eye, become aware of Jesus entering the room. Imagine him in any way that feels comfortable to you. Jesus sits in a chair beside you. He takes your hand in his. With your fingers, you can trace the nail print in his hand. Deep peace comes from him. His love warms your hand. The healing warmth flows up through your hand into your arm, warming you, healing you. That warmth now calms the muscles of your shoulder. The warmth of his love fills your chest and surrounds your heart. Rest there a while, and be still and at peace in Jesus' presence.

Next, Jesus speaks to you quietly and tenderly. In a whisper he tells you, "I want you to know it is safe, so very safe, to be here with me. As you feel ready, one by one tell me some of the stresses and worries that weigh you down." Tell him about your stresses and worries.

DISCUSSION QUESTIONS

1. What are some of the parables Jesus told or some of his sermons that make use of the imagination?
2. From TV commercials to billboards, advertisers try to hijack our imaginations. They want to dose your unconscious with imaginative scenes that will encourage you to buy their products. What are some of these advertising images that you can think of?
3. In the guided prayer, what did it feel like when Jesus took your hand?

CHAPTER 5

How God's love can lift depression

Maria smiled broadly when she shook my hand. I saw vigor in her I had hardly believed was possible when I led the first retreat at her parish two years earlier.

When I had initially met her during that first retreat, her body seemed weighed down with a great load, and desperation shone in her eyes.

Maria was so depressed she could no longer hide it.

She came up to talk with me after I finished giving the first talk on the first night of the retreat.

We went to a side chapel where she said haltingly, "I just

can't keep going on. I want to quit."

"Quit what?" I asked.

"Quit life," she sighed.

Then the tears, seemingly unstoppable, burst out of her eyes.
She had to leave in just a moment to pick up her 13-year-
old son from his Christian education class going on simultane-
ously in the adjacent building and we only had a few minutes
to talk, so I asked her the most important question I ask of
everyone who comes to me so burdened.

"Do you have any thoughts of harming yourself?"

"Thoughts like that may pass through my mind, but I know I
couldn't do that to my family," she said. "Good," I said. "Do you
think you could briefly tell me what is wrong?"

As she wiped her eye with a tissue, she said, "Life no longer
has joy for me. Everything seems meaningless. I feel dead inside."

I arranged for her to meet me for a longer session the next
afternoon.

There, her labored words came out slowly. "I lost my job as
a teacher when budget deficits caused the school system to cut
back on personnel.

"At first my husband, Todd, and I rejoiced. Todd, as an emer-
gency room physician, brings in more than enough money for
our family. I could stay home and make a great home for our
two teenage boys and engage in my real love—creative writing. I wanted to break into writing by publishing several short
stories for mystery magazines.

"I found, however, when I stayed home every day the bot-
tom fell out. I stared at blank computer screens and the words
and ideas didn't come for my short stories. I didn't even feel

like keeping the house or cooking, and my husband had to hire a part-time maid. I tried substitute teaching to get out of the house, but I felt so down I couldn't concentrate on teaching and had to quit. When the school system started hiring again, I couldn't get the energy again to fill out an application.

"I don't know what more I can do. Life just has no meaning."

It was clear in talking with her that losing her job was just a trigger. Maria had an underlying depression ready to show itself even before that. Her feelings of despair were out of proportion to the life events that triggered the depression.

I responded, "It seems to me you are seriously depressed. You have an illness, depression, and depression is one of the most treatable of serious illnesses. It's important for you to get treatment right away."

She replied, "I had always thought of myself as a good person. What bad thing have I done to sink this low?"

I assured her, "Depression is not a character flaw. Usually there is an underlying biochemical imbalance, which, often along with negative thinking, causes the depression. The MRIs of depressed people show significant differences with those who are not depressed. You are likely dealing, at least in part, with something physical."

I looked at her in the eye and softly said to her, "No way, Maria, are you to blame. You have an illness like diabetes or heart disease."

"What steps do I take?" she asked.

"First, go to your physician and tell him about your depression. He will most likely want to run some tests to rule out other illnesses that sometimes mimic depression—like thyroid problems.

"Next, seek out a counselor. Your diocesan Catholic social services should have several counselors available. Seek out one with whom you are comfortable. He or she will likely refer you back to your physician or a psychiatrist to get a prescription antidepressant. Antidepressants are to depression what insulin is to diabetes. They help balance the chemicals in the brain and in the nervous system.

"Your pastor mentioned to me that the counselors at Catholic Social Services are all trained in cognitive therapy, a therapy that helps people turn negative thoughts into realistic thoughts. It has been proven as effective as medication for depression and, combined with medication, highly likely to heal and cure.

"And remember to pray. Dosing yourself daily with God's love will speed your recovery."

I gave her a copy of a book I wrote called *Letters from Jesus*, a devotional guide that helps the reader open up daily to the tender love of God. I gave her my phone number and told her to call me anytime.

I heard from her several times over the next two years. She went to the Catholic counselor and started on antidepressant medication. She improved rapidly. She had a new sense of purpose; life took on great meaning. She told me that the prayer helped as much as the medical treatment.

Not all sadness is as severe as Maria's or requires the same level of medical intervention. We all get the blues at times—situational sadness. However, whether the sadness is transitory or entrenched, God can help.

A study released by Rush University Medical Center in Chicago found that among those diagnosed with clinical depression, "belief in a concerned God can improve response to medical treatment." The study published by the *Journal of Clinical Psychology* affirms what the Scriptures already tell us—God can help.

The first step in seeking God's help is to simply ask him. He is ready to help the moment we call on him. But we need to humble ourselves and ask. Matthew 7:11 tells us how anxious God is to help: "If you then...know how to give good gifts to your children, how much more will your Father in heaven give good things to those who ask him!"

Like many others, I find the psalms a great aid in dealing with sadness and inner pain. Over and over again the psalmist articulates the pain to God, who is so anxious to help the crushed in spirit. The psalmist is humble enough to ask for God's help.

Like the psalmist, we need to articulate our negative thoughts and inner pain to God. If it is big enough to bother me, it is big enough for me to take to God. The very act of giving despairing feelings a name takes away much of their sting.

We need to say prayers such as this: "For we sink down to the dust; our bodies cling to the ground. Rise up, come to our help. Redeem us for the sake of your steadfast love" (Ps 44:25–26).

The psalmist tells us that God cares about each tear we shed. We need only call on him and he will manifest his comforting Presence.

"You have kept count of my tossings; put my tears in your bottle. Are they not in your record?" (Ps 56:8).

God hears our cries and God helps. "This poor soul cried, and was heard by the Lord, and was saved from every trouble" (Ps 34:6).

When sadness overtakes me, I often find that it helps enormously to write out my feelings as a prayer to God. Keep a sadness journal in which you pour out your despair on paper and write God prayers.

Healing prayer, opening yourself to the touch of God's love daily, starts you on the road to recovery.

Prayer experience

Take time to relax and be still. Repeat a short prayer phrase. Picture yourself surrounded by God's presence in the form of light that encircles you. If your imagination is fuzzy, just have the sense that you are surrounded by invisible light. You don't have to picture the light with precision to enter into the mystery of it. A sense of being surrounded by light is enough.

The warm light of God's love absorbs your negative and crushed emotions like a sponge. The light richly relaxes and refreshes you. You tingle with newness. The light tells you in a beautiful, eternal way beyond words of God's immense, unfathomable, tender, and special love for you. Rest for a long time, sensing yourself bathed in his light.

After you are comfortable in the light, begin to be aware of your breathing in and your breathing out. The word for the Holy Spirit in Scripture is also the word for breathe. Allow your breathing in and out to remind you of the Holy Spirit. Just notice your breathing.

Now have a sense every time you breathe in that you are breathing in the light that surrounds you. As you breathe it in, a warm, glowing center grows in the depths of your chest, warming your heart. The more you breathe in the light, the more the center of your chest glows, relaxing you, healing you, warming your being with God's love. Each time you exhale, have a sense that you are breathing out negativity and fear. Each time you inhale, you are breathing in light.

Take as long as you like breathing in the love of God.

DISCUSSION QUESTIONS

1. What do you think the difference is between transitory sadness and clinical depression?
2. What are some of the ways you could help a friend or relative going through depression?
3. Why do you think praying the psalms can be such a help in times of depression?
4. How does articulating your pain to God help?

✳ CHAPTER 6 ✳

Healing after events of mindless violence

like Newtown or Columbine

H orror, shock, and sorrow: these emotions come to mind whenever I hear of the latest scene of senseless slaughter. Whether it is at the movies in Aurora or at Sandy Hook School in Newtown or some other unexpected place, it affects me; really, it affects all of us.

Ten years ago a tragedy like that happened near me. Once,

when my mind turned to the old site of Christ the King Parish, near the hamlet of Hamilton, GA, I thought of peace, safety, and beauty. Nestled on a mountain road winding its way toward the famous Callaway Gardens, it was a charming setting for the many happy retreats I had led for youth and children from our Columbus Deanery.

Now instead of peace I experience a tumble of feelings. It will be a while before I can envision that place with a sense of peace. Though not on the scale of Newtown, Aurora, Columbine, or other scenes of the butchery of innocents, the events that began for the two nuns in that mobile home shook the small community of Catholics in the Columbus Deanery to the quick and threw me into a tumultuous grief that I am still, on a lower decibel level, working my way through.

I still myself, close my eyes, make the Sign of the Cross, and say a prayer when I pass by that old scene.

When the news came

I was busily leading a parish retreat 800 miles away in a suburb of Detroit when my 90-year-old mother called. In a quiet, shaky voice she asked me what I thought of Sister Philomena's murder. My first reaction was unbelief. I hadn't even heard of her murder, being so far away from the local media.

"Are you sure you have the facts right, Mother?" I responded. Mother didn't seem to have details.

The very idea was unspeakable, unimaginable.

Looking for more specifics, I immediately got on the Internet and looked up news articles that told the story that began four days earlier. As I read I felt as though I were slipping down into the shadows of a bottomless hole.

The next morning I was on the phone with my close friend and confidant Deacon John Quillen, the deacon at Christ the King. My co-worker Deacon Robert Herrmann talked to Ann Pinkney, another friend of Sister Philomena's and mine.

The story that emerged from these articles and phone calls seemed unreal.

Adrian Robinson, in his late twenties, son of Christ the King parishioner Henry Robinson, shot his father 16 times and left him dead.

He then broke into the sisters' mobile home on the site and abducted them at gunpoint. He put Sister Philomena in the trunk of the sisters' own car and Sister Lucie in the front seat. He then drove to Norfolk, Virginia, 560 miles away.

Adrian checked the three of them into a hotel room. He then started to take Sister Philomena out of the room. She must somehow have known his intentions because as they left the room she told him three times, "Adrian, I forgive you."

After the two left, Sr. Lucie was able to unbind herself and summon help.

They found Philomena's decapitated and mutilated body in a parking lot and a few hours later arrested Adrian.

Away from our base of support, St. Anne in Columbus, GA, Deacon Robert and I first had to wrestle with our feelings by ourselves.

The first and major feeling I had to deal with was the utter loss; a precious life that had touched thousands was snuffed out senselessly.

The Mother Teresa of Harris County

When you ask local people about Sister Phil the first word that comes from people's mouth is "saint." Then the phrase "She was the Mother Teresa of Harris County" usually follows. She was small of stature, but had the heart of a giant. Her life and work had impacted thousands of people. She headed an ecumenical ministry to the marginalized, poor, and elderly of Harris County. She counseled inmates at the jail. It didn't matter if you were Catholic, Baptist, Pentecostal, or atheist; if you needed help, Sister Philomena was there to help.

The neat and clean clothes Philomena wore came straight from the clothes rack for the disadvantaged. If some of us bought new clothes for her to wear, she would immediately sell them and give the money to an elderly person who needed money to pay a utility bill or some other cause for the poor.

I had known Sister Phil for more than a decade. She was always there whenever I led a retreat at the Christ the King site. She was a strong personality, and I stood in awe of her care for "the least of these."

For her, no one was beyond God's love.

Loss is communal, as well as personal

The tragedy I faced was faced by all the Catholics in our deanery, as well as people of many faith persuasions throughout Harris County and Columbus.

Thrown into grief, we all walked through that dark valley the old spiritual speaks about.

The people of Aurora, Littleton, Newtown, and so many other sites have confronted similar struggles. All of us, whether we live near a site of senseless massacre or have simply heard about it through the media, have had to muddle through deep waters. A verse from Lamentations sums it up, "Happiness has

gone out of our lives, Grief has taken the place of our dances"
(Lam 5:15).

Something I felt for a while and I think that most of the people in my deanery also felt is the fragility of us all. The unspeakable can happen to any of us anytime or to anyone whom we
hold tenderly. The safest of places, the most innocent among
us, can be caught up in horror.

Several months after Philomena's death, one of the moth-
ers at my own parish of St. Anne told me that she dreaded the
possibility that an intruder could unalterably change her life if
St. Anne's School, which her third grader attended, or her husband's work place became the next place of carnage.

Violence impacts all of us

We are all affected, even if the site of the killings is a thousand miles away. Stories that get heavy media attention, such
as Columbine and Newtown, unsettle us all on some level. If it
happened to them, it can happen to us or our dear ones. Such
stories disquiet most of us in our depths. When these senseless
tragedies happen, we all need healing.

The first thing we can do when we hear of such a scene is
open to God. Take a moment and say a prayer. It doesn't matter
what prayer; all that matters is that you pray. You can especially
pray that the healing warmth of God descend on all involved.

The next thing we can do is give of ourselves to others. When
the pastor at St. Rose of Lima in Newtown was faced with 11
funerals, 20 to 30 other priests joined with him in comforting
the grieving and personally supporting him in the midst of the
dread.

One of the first things that the Christ the King parishioners did after the murder of Sister Philomena was to reach out to the Robinson family. Even though it was a member of that family who committed the murders, the parishioners surrounded them with love, comfort, and help. It was what Philomena would have wanted.

Deacon Robert, who was also grieving, helped support me despite his own loss. Away from my support community and leading a mission in Michigan, I said nothing to the congregation about the murders. My role was to give them a retreat, not to plunge them into my grief. I waited till after the mission's final blessing; then told them about Philomena and the abduction. I recounted how heroic she had been for the gospel.

The congregation responded with hugs; tears mingled with mine and prayers were offered. A burden lifted from me that night.

When the violence comes close

In the long term, another thing a community hit by violence can do is build a memorial. The process of raising the funds, designing, and building the Columbine memorial drew people together and sped them along a heart-mending pathway.

The first memorial Catholics in our area raised for Sister Philomena was a spiritual one: to save Adrian from the death penalty. Despite the gravity of the loss, Catholics in our area wrote authorities in Virginia urging them to spare Adrian, who was mentally ill. Sister Lucie, who was also abducted, testified at Adrian's trial, asking that Adrian be spared the death penalty. All our prayers were answered when Adrian was sentenced to life without possibility of parole.

Later, a house, dubbed Philomena House, was bought to carry on Sister Phil's extraordinary work with the disadvantaged.

When you lose someone to violence

Recovering from such tragedies is, of course, grief experience.

While we are all affected by senseless violence, those who lose a loved one to violence suffer in unimaginable ways.

But in a way, hearing about these mass killings from a distance can cause the pain of our own losses to throb.

If you have a loved one who died from heart disease, cancer, or some other natural cause, it can seem like violence.

An alternate word for grief is "bereaved"—a violent word. The dictionary says it means "to be ravaged, plundered, torn." Someone we cherish has been torn from us.

As my friend, grief counselor, and author Judy Esway writes in St. Anthony Messenger, "The grief we feel is the natural consequence of love, and the greater our love the greater the grief."

C.S. Lewis wrote, "The pain now is part of the happiness then. That's the deal."

At first our grief may be pure, sorrow, tears. But for many of us complications come in.

Grief expert Brian Mclaren suggests several possible complications. Guilt is one: "I wish I had told the one I lost how much I loved him."

At Christ the King, the faith and holiness of Sister Philomena helped keep the grieving pure, less cluttered by thoughts of revenge, regret, and guilt.

That was not true for me, however. I don't think I ever doubted Sister Philomena's goodness or her dedication as a religious, but my relationship with her was complicated. I had all the good memories of working with her on retreats, but clouds had come into my relationship with her. For nearly four years she was the facilitator in my Loyola University learning group. We met weekly for discussion and sharing. Sister Phil and I had different temperaments. Also, we were both strong personalities and clashed in class several times. I let anger burrow its way into my heart.

A couple of years before her death I went to her with tears in my eyes to ask her forgiveness. She attended my ordination and made a gift for me she crafted herself.

Upon hearing of her death, guilt welled up inside me. I wanted to tell her how much I appreciated her sacrificial love to the whole community. I wanted to tell her I loved her.

I slept uneasily after her death. Then one night I dreamed vividly that she came to me surrounded by light. She told me that she was fine and that things were good between us.

Such healing dreams of a loved one or just a sense of his or her presence often comes after loss. They can be like a sign of hope sent by God.

Anger is another complication: "If only the doctor had taken better care." Fear is another: "Will I feel this way forever?"

Denial is still another: "I can't take the time to struggle with this; I'll just try to think of something else."

Brian Mclaren writes: "Grief is important. It should not be bypassed. It flows from the way God made us in his image, to cherish and appreciate every good thing. And we have to grieve when it is taken away. The apostle Paul said, 'We do not grieve as those who have no hope.'"

HEALING PRAYER EXPERIENCE

Sit comfortably. Perhaps put on some stilling music. Let the love of God sweep over you. In your imagination Jesus stands near you and says, "You are safe, so very safe in my presence. You can tell me what is in your heart. We are going to explore violence. I suffered and died violently and I take upon me all the violence of the world. When you talk about violence, I know what you are talking about."

Jesus asks you to think of some of the feelings you have after you hear of an event of violence.

He then hands you an old-fashioned tablet with big lines. He asks you to print out in large letters, like you used to print when you were little, the name of a feeling you have when news comes to you of senseless violence. You finish writing the name of the feeling and hand it to Jesus. He takes it reverently and presses it to his heart. The paper—the feeling—disappear into his heart. Do this several times for several feelings.

He now tells you, "Now when you feel these feelings, know that they are linked to my heart and whenever you feel them, the feeling also stirs in me. You never have to feel them alone; I feel them with you."

Jesus now places his hand on your chest. He says, "I plant peace inside you. Whenever stressful emotions about violence emerge in you, you will begin to feel this peace. This peace will grow inside you, transforming the feelings of pain to emblems of hope."

Jesus then says to you, "Let me show you something." He holds up a globe of the world, surrounding it with the visible light of his love. The globe turns into an orb of light. He says, "I hold this world in my heart. What was lost will be restored. What was torn apart will be put back together. My new creation absorbs all pain, transfiguring it in my sacred heart."

In your own words you respond by saying a prayer of thanksgiving.

DISCUSSION QUESTIONS

1. What were some of the feelings you wrote on the tablet sheets?
2. What does the phrase "new creation" mean to you?
3. What are some ways you and your parish can reach out to those touched by violence?
4. Suggestion: Brainstorm among yourselves and write a common prayer of thanksgiving to the God who will bring together that which was torn asunder.

CHAPTER 7

Healing from pornography addiction

Addictions can hold us, imprison us. Often we don't see a way out. If you have a problem with pornography, turning to this chapter is a reaching out, an admission you need help. You have made a big stride just by reading this. If you turned to this chapter because someone you love is trapped by pornography, you have made a step toward resolution.

Have hope; there is a way out. Through God's help and the

help of others there is a way to break the cycle.

Starting with casual interest, both men and women can stay up hours each night, while the spouse and the rest of the family sleep soundly, gazing at raw, distorted images of sexuality. Sometimes it can seem like there is no hope. You want to quit, but somehow you can't stop watching.

Before the Internet, someone might pull down a hat over the face, make a trip to the red light district of town, and sneak away with a magazine or two.

Now it is easy to anonymously access millions of dark images after one or two clicks on the computer.

People who access porn on the web are not shady strangers from a different side of town; they are lawyers, mechanics, school teachers, executives, a parishioner next to you in a pew—people who, to all appearances, seem to easily blend in. And it is not just a men's problem One survey in *Today's Christian Woman* found that one in six women were addicted to porn, including Christian believers.

This addiction takes a terrible toll on marriages, families, friendships, and at the work place.

In the face of pornography addiction, marriages can crumble and families fall apart.

I was leading a parish retreat out west. As I looked out over the congregation, a man, Rick, who looked to be in his mid-forties, seemed as interested as anyone in my talk on God's grace. Then time came for silent prayer, waiting in the stillness for God to pour down his love upon us, time to sense Jesus coming to us and taking our hand.

His face became contorted; his muscles almost seized up, so great was his distress. Afterward, with his face and body radiating fear, he came up to me and said, "We have to talk."

"Fine with me," I responded. I wondered if he was working through some bad memory from childhood.

I took us to a side chapel and his fears tumbled out. "I can't keep away from explicit pictures of women, even violent sexual images of women. I thought the prayer would help but in the contemplative silence all I saw were those sexual images. While I was supposed to be imagining Jesus, these images paraded by. Ever since I have been hooked on porn, every time I stop to pray, those dark images flood me. What can I do?"

I knew I had only a short amount of time with him, so I was direct, rather than just reflectively listening. "You have been incredibly courageous today; you reached out and told me, another person, about your predicament. Dear friend, God doesn't condemn you; don't condemn yourself. He is an incredibly merciful and tender God. Take all this to him and you will find help."

I quoted Romans 8:1: There is therefore now no condemnation for those who are in Christ Jesus. "You seem to be carrying a grand canyon full of guilt on your shoulders," I told him.

"I am," he replied.

"Our God, through Christ, is a lavish forgiver. Like a parent he kisses our offenses into everlasting forgetfulness.

"As soon as you can, read the entire eighth chapter of Romans and make an act of contrition. If you can't make a spontaneous act of contrition, there are cards with an act of contrition over by the confessional. Next, make an appointment with a trusted priest in the area for the sacrament of reconciliation. Ask the priest about further resources in the community. I understand a neighboring parish has a sexual addictions support group.

Hard as it may seem, go there with fellow strugglers who are honest to each other. I also think you are so caught up in these images, professional help may be needed. Ask the priest you see for a referral. If he doesn't know of anyone especially qualified to help, go to your diocesan social services and ask for a referral.

"Don't expect your problems to go away overnight. It took time to become addicted; it will take time to get out of addiction."

I saw a glimmer of hope cross his eyes as I talked.

He then asked me, "You said prayer is so important. I can't even pray. What do I do?"

"First of all, prayer is a healing medicine for this kind of addiction. It fills your heart with holy and healthy images, not dark ones. If it is too hard for you to pray spontaneously, find a prayer book and read the prayers. If the images start flooding you, keep reading and praying despite them. Don't let them stop you from praying. Also get a picture of Jesus, one where his compassion shines forth. Gaze at that picture; implant it in your mind till you can see it with your eyes closed. Then imagine the picture of Jesus descending into your heart."

I handed him a holy card with this prayer from Saint Augustine and suggested he read it every night before falling asleep:

> *Breathe in me, Holy Spirit,*
> > *that all my thoughts may be holy,*
> *Act in me, Holy Spirit,*
> > *that my work, too, may be holy,*
> *Draw my heart, Holy Spirit,*
> > *that I may love only what is holy,*

> *Strengthen me, Holy Spirit,*
> *to defend all that is holy,*
> *Guard me, Holy Spirit, that I may always be holy.*

He talked some more. "My wife just found out a week ago. She found some of the hidden files on my computer. She confronted me. I denied it. For the last few days we have just slammed doors. We were having big trouble even before she found out. I had grown so distant from her. What do I do?"

"After you have gone to the sacrament of reconciliation, go to your wife," I said. "Tell her the truth. Tell her you are struggling and taking the steps needed to get help. Ask her forgiveness. I don't know, but I somehow suspect that that forgiveness will be given."

I gave him my card and told him he could call me anytime in Georgia when I was home. I heard from him once. He and his wife were making steady progress in healing their relationship. He was part of a support group and seeing a Catholic professional counselor. I said a prayer of thanksgiving.

Some problems with pornography are not as grave as Rick's. For some, pornography is borderline. I know of a woman who collected pictures of men in bathing suits on her computer, but she looked at them lustfully. Lately she had added several fully nude images. In her case my advice was that this could turn into a grave addiction over time. I suggested she go to the sacrament of reconciliation and try to change her environment.

It's good advice for anyone struggling with pornography. Put the computer in full view of everyone, not just in your office or some unused room. Knowing others may see you will be a great help. Make a resolution to use your computer only for workplace-related needs. If you find yourself stumbling from this resolution, pick yourself up and try again. It's a journey toward freedom, not usually a onetime event.

The transformation of our sexuality

The channeling or transformation of our sexuality that comes from our closeness to God changes our desires. We see the beauty of God's love in sexually attractive persons. Rather than wanting to consume, possess, or exploit them, we see them as gentle channels of God's presence; we look upon them with a contemplative gaze. Saint John Climacus, an early church father and saint, describes this:

> *A certain man, seeing a woman of unusual beauty, glorified the Creator for her; the mere sight of her moved him to love God and made him shed a flood of tears. It was indeed astonishing to see how what for another could have been a pitfall to perdition was for him the supernatural cause of crown of glory. If such a man, on similar occasions, feels and acts in the same way, he is risen, and is incorruptible, even before the general resurrection.*

GUIDED PRAYER EXPERIENCES

Planting wholesome pictures in the depths of our heart of loving and tenderness can help drive out and replace the darker images. The following meditation is not just for those who need to replace darkness, but for anyone wanting to channel sexual urges into compassion and disinterested agape love.

Part 1 Imagine that you are the woman who is anointing Jesus' feet with ointment and with tears. Tenderly caress and kiss his feet. Feel only the feelings you choose to feel. It might be tenderness, tinged with joy. Feel this tenderness as a small spiral of light spinning around you, flowing out to those in need. Picture yourself loving other people with the same tenderness, especially those whose poverty and pain are all too real.

Part 2 Unless, on some level, we imagine and practice what Jesus would do, how can we follow in his steps and take on the mind of Christ? So, imagine that you are Jesus and that your feet are being anointed and kissed tenderly. How do you feel?

Now feel this tenderness like a small spinning spiral of light surrounding you, flowing out to those who need that love. Picture yourself loving others with the same tenderness, especially those who suffer poverty and pain.

DISCUSSION QUESTIONS

1. What was it like to be the one anointing and washing Jesus' feet?
2. What was it like to be the one having your feet anointed?
3. What are some wholesome avenues for the human ability to be caring, affectionate, and compassionate?
4. How can closeness to God help us stay away from pornography?

✳ CHAPTER 8 ✳

Healing when a child is different

Bill and Ruth and their daughter and son-in-law, along with my co-worker Deacon Robert Herrmann and I, had a joyous reunion at a restaurant one evening when we passed through Bill and Ruth's home town of San Antonio. I had known Bill and Ruth for over 40 years, back as far as when they were students in Austin, Texas, while I studied there at the Presbyterian seminary before becoming Catholic. Bill is an especially caring person who was studying to be a social worker at St. Edward's University in Austin. I suffered from then undiagnosed right hemisphere brain dysfunction, also known as non-verbal learning disabilities: simple tasks of living were confusing to me and I didn't know why. Bill helped me with many of these daily tasks even though then we did not know the cause of the problem. He was a steady, comforting presence who did far more to help me than any friend could be expected to do. He had helped carry me through a difficult time in my life. My co-worker, Deacon Robert Herrmann, graciously plays much of that same role in my life today.

When we finished supper we set out for Bill's car so he could return us to the hotel where we were staying. I left the restaurant and walked out to what I thought was his car. It was really a different colored car, far from Bill's car. Even seeing everyone else in our group head toward Bill's actual car, I still had gotten lost, a symptom of my disorder. They shouted at me and waved to me to come to the right car. When I got there Bill put his hand on my shoulder, laughing along with everyone else as I laughed with them. "Eddie, you are a joy," he said. And Deacon Robert added "and a lot of fun." They had seen me get lost like that many times, and what was once fearful for me, I and my friends now took lightly.

Back when I was a child and young man, outright terror and shame were my responses to my disability, which had not yet been diagnosed. I had little ability to organize or focus, and my handwriting was illegible. Math—and science that used math—gave me problems. I had poor social skills and difficulty following instructions, both symptoms of learning disability. Yet, my left hemisphere, the part of that brain that controls language and logic, worked overtime. I excelled at reading and had a phenomenal ability to express myself in words. Because of this, some mistakenly considered me a near genius. Since my grades were often mediocre or failing, teachers, and even at times my parents, called me lazy, careless, and slovenly. I carried a load of disgrace and guilt with me constantly. I remember the deep look of disappointment in my parents' eyes when I failed at tasks yet again.

Yet, whenever I took time for prayer, especially the prayer of resting in God's love, the shame would disappear for a while. In the center of my heart I would receive a whispered assurance that things would work out and that God had a plan for me. After a thoroughgoing work-up at a brain injury center 20 years ago, I received my diagnosis. The professionals there said they didn't know how someone with so much impairment had finished high school, much less graduated from college, and written two books. Silently, I said to myself, I know how. I had a master encourager—God. Receiving appropriate accommodations for my impairment, I went on to earn a master's degree in pastoral studies and a doctorate in clinical pastoral counseling and wrote six more books.

The day of my diagnosis was the day of my liberation. I finally understood my problem, and the shame and guilt slowly began to slip away.

God works through ordinary means, too. I learned computers during a year of outpatient rehab for my condition. For people with right hemisphere brain damage, computers are a miracle. On a computer I don't have to switch sensory modalities and can organize and plan well.

Educators and psychologists who have researched the subject estimate 15 percent of the public has a learning disability or ADHD.

Most who suffer from those conditions have normal overall intelligence or, in many cases, are exceptionally bright.

Dyslexia, Asperger's, which is a mild form of autism that is similar to nonverbal learning disabilities, ADHD, Nonverbal Learning Disabilities, and other forms of neurological disorders abound among children in our culture. Only in the last 30 years have clinicians and educators been able to identify, accommodate, and treat these disorders on a wide scale. No one with such a condition should ever feel impaired potential.

We love our children. We want them to be normal. We want them to fit in. But some children are born with one or more of these disabilities, and it can make school and life at home difficult. If you already have a diagnosis, prayer and spirituality can help you cope and can guide you to the best possible outcome for your child.

Most children with these disorders are bright; they just learn differently.

The child often suffers emotionally and often socially. "I just don't fit in," as one child with non-verbal learning disabilities told me.

Perhaps you are an adult who still is challenged by these difficulties. Healing prayer can help heal the wounds of the past and brighten your future. Perhaps you are a teenager struggling with such a disability; prayer can help you.

Prayer, meditation, and spirituality can help you cope.

Healing meditations can help give you the confidence to advocate for your child or, if you are the one who has the disability, advocate for yourself for the right accommodations.

Grace builds upon the natural. If you suspect your child or you have a learning disability, seek out professional testing to confirm it.

Then, as in the case of a child, seek appropriate accommodations at school—different testing formats, extra time on tests, and help in taking notes.

Your child is probably carrying a ton of shame. Over and over again, build your child's confidence; explain that he or she can learn well, just differently.

If you are the one with the disability, meditating on the compassion that comes from the center of Eternity, God himself, helps heal the scars of shame, rejection, or guilt. A bright future can open up before you.

PRAYER EXPERIENCES

Part 1 Shame goes with these learning disorders—often years of built-up shame. This prayer experience is meant for you if you have a learning disorder or for you to read to your child who has a learning disorder.

Take a few minutes to relax. Imagine that you are in a wondrous place, a special place. You are on a huge, beautiful beach of white, powdery sand. A vast ocean stretches out before you. You are lying on the beach with your feet in the water. Hear the sound of the crashing whitecaps. Smell the salt air as it fills your nostrils. Hear the gulls squawking as they glide high above the sea.

The water is warm. The waves begin to break over you. You realize that this is a special ocean; this is the ocean of God's love. It is endless. Feel the waves breaking over your whole body, one after the other. The water is warm and healing. It is as though the waves flow not only on your outside, but on your inside too. They go right through you, their gentle motion carrying away anxiety, tension, and shame. Each wave coming in fills you with joy. Each wave going out takes away shame and guilt. Those waves tell you without words of God's love. They leave you deeply peaceful.

Rest for as long as you wish on the beach, allowing the waves of God's love to sweep over you and heal you.

Part 2   Now that you are deeply relaxed, recall a scene when a teacher, fellow student, or family member ridiculed you for your disability. Standing beside you is Jesus, holding you in his arm. You can feel the healing warmth of his arm around you, stilling you and bringing you great peace. Now hear the words of ridicule; look at the scornful facial expressions. Jesus holds you tighter and whispers in your ear, "None of this is true; you are my own child and with my help you can do great things."

DISCUSSION QUESTIONS

1. What is it like to let shame go from our lives?
2. Can you think of a child with a learning disorder who went on to excel? Tell the story.
3. What can you do in your parish and your parish's religious education program to better understand children with learning disorders?

CHAPTER 9

Putting the family back together

So many forces in today's world tend to pull families apart. With busy schedules, meals can be hurried or eaten in front of the television. Rushing off to good things like soccer practice or dance class can still keep families from enjoying time together.

It can be so easy for each family member to live in a separate reality, easy for each family member to focus on his or her self. With the advent of the Internet and other electronic media, family members can develop virtual relationships while neglecting the human and holy relationships within families.

With so much going on, husband and wife can have little time left to be a couple. Single parents can almost lose a sense of their own identity. Anger, loneliness, and pain can result from such a scattered existence.

Not only do "everyday things" tend to pull today's families in different directions; heavy exposure to the media can send all sorts of mistaken messages. Many voices in our broader society tell us that what are important are individual achievement, power, and affluence. The media often highlight rage and violence as acceptable and encourage us to use people and revere things.

If families are being pulled apart by the media and by busyness, they may even fracture, leading to possible divorce and causing the children to get snared in unhealthy life trajectories.

Most families yearn for more than this. They want to be closer, to love each other more, and to make memories that will be cherished. They want families to be sacred—not just a gathering of individuals under one roof, but a true family in the fullest meaning of that word. But how do we recapture the sacredness of families? How do we celebrate faith in this environment?

The beginning point is to realize that families are indeed sacred and called to holiness. God created families; they are dear to him. God means for families to be a refuge from whatever storms might be blowing outside, a school of compassion and self-giving, and a nurturing place in which to grow up. Faithful families root themselves in the depths of God's love. God is the one who fills families with love and faith. There are, however, important ways families can cooperate with God.

Make time

Taking a short time each day for family devotionals is a wonderful means of celebrating faith. Read short passages from Scripture and take time for any family member who wants to say a prayer. Soon family devotions can become a sacred center of togetherness. Also, be sure and say grace together before meals.

Making time for silence is one of the most important things families can do. Here, in the stillness, our hearts are knit with God's and with each others. Family expert James Merhaut tells us: "All paths to holiness begin with silence, and so it must be an essential part of family faith formation. God communicates directly to the human heart without the medium of language." In the silence, God expresses the tenderness of his love and calms us.

One family I know personally began to consciously cultivate silence at family devotions. Besides the parents, the family included an 11-year-old daughter, a 14-year-old son, and an 8-year-old son. After a Scripture passage was read and each family member had a chance to pray out loud, a candle would be lit and the family would sit in silent prayer for five or six minutes. In those silences, God, who comes in the stillness too deep for words, tied their hearts together. After the silence, each member of the family had a chance to say in a sentence or two what was in their hearts. Simple and profound words would pour forth. In one case after the silence, the mother, who had lost her temper earlier in the day, simply said a heartfelt, "Please forgive me." Other times, members would say words such as, "It's been a good day," or "God is good to us." The silent time and the words that came after profoundly bound the family together.

Group silence reminds us that the experience of God is not so much taught as caught. Quaker theologian Rufus Jones tells how, as a child, he learned to experience God through the contagion of being near people who felt God. Each day his family took time for silence together. Furthermore, as a child he attended regular silent prayer sessions in which people disposed themselves to the One Love. He wrote, "There was something contagious about the silence...There was a touch of awe and majesty, of surprise and wonder...there was a gleam of eternal reality breaking on the humble group."

We don't have to turn our homes into monasteries to experience the graces of silence and space. Here are some suggestions for creating that space:

1. Turn off the television and all telephones during meal times. Family meals should be limited to conversation, not more noise.

2. Make sure that family members fall asleep without music or watching television. Become accustomed to falling asleep in the midst of the natural sounds of the country or an urban area.

3. Encourage family nature walks in nearby parks or woods.

4. Don't overbook the children with sports, lessons, etc. Let the family have what Merhaut calls "down time"—time just to be children and family.

Everyday sacred moments

God comes to us in the everyday happenings of life: comfort after loss, reconciliation after estrangement. At times God seems to break through in the most unexpected ways. Theologian John Shea, in his book *An Experience Named Spirit*, writes:

> *...there are moments which, although they occur within the everyday confines of human living, take*

on larger meaning. They have a lasting impact; they cut through to something deeper; they demand a hearing. It might be the death of a parent, the touch of a friend, a betrayal...whatever it is, we sense we have undergone something that has touched upon the normally dormant but always present relationship with God.

Families can take time to actively remember and talk about such moments of meaning. Also, they can tie such moments to faith history, the story of God coming to his people over the centuries in the Bible, and explore their meaning for the life of the family.

Consciously nurture compassion

Jan Johnson writes, "Teaching kids to care for people beyond their backyard is one more way to teach our children to love God." We need to teach our children to partner with an all-loving God to reach out to others. One set of parents I know suggested to their children that one summer, instead of a beach vacation, the family go on a church-sponsored mission trip to rural Mexico to install a clean water filter in the local well.

At first, their teenage son objected, but soon after they got there, he loved working hard and being in a different culture. He enjoyed it so much that when he finished his first year of college, he volunteered to spend his entire summer in Haiti, helping in a medical clinic. Nurturing compassion gives a family a deep sense of purpose beyond itself.

Celebrating faith in a world seemingly too busy to care can seem like quite a chore. It's not, however, if we let God do the heavy lifting. His comforting, nurturing love can accompany us each step of the way. As individuals and families, we were built to encounter God. Our true purpose is found only in relationship to him. Abiding in his love as a family transfigures us.

GUIDED PRAYER EXPERIENCE

Let yourself grow still and let the warmth of God's healing love flow through you. Allow the muscles of your face to grow loose and relaxed in his presence. The muscles of your neck and shoulder grow limp and relaxed because of God's nearness. Your back and spine feel the warmth of his love. The muscles of your stomach become calm and relaxed; the muscles of your upper legs let go of tension. Your lower legs and feet grow heavy with holy relaxation.

Rest a few moments in the warmth and stillness of his presence.

Godly relaxation enables us all to remember so much more vividly. Just as the rosary has its sorrowful and joyful mysteries, so do our lives. It's time to remember some of your joyful mysteries, joyful memories.

Think of a time when you and your family had an experience that was sacred that drew you together. Perhaps it was a scene in nature such as the shore, the mountains, or the Grand Canyon, perhaps a time you prayed together as a family.

It could perhaps be a time of shared grief in which everyone keenly felt how much they loved each other and loved God. Let your mind recall such times.

Now let your mind's eye turn to your family in the here and now. Has this busy world been pulling you apart?

Now imagine your current family gathered together in a

circle, reciting a decade of the rosary, reading Scripture, or sitting calmly in contemplative silence. What does that scene look like?

Now envision Jesus joining that circle. Jesus and your whole family hold hands. The light from his presence now surrounds all of you in a cocoon of loving light. While in the circle, you ask Jesus what your family can do to become a holier family. What does he say?

DISCUSSION QUESTIONS

1. When you remembered your childhood, what sacred scene did you remember?
2. How can you help usher such moments into the life of your current family?
3. What did Jesus say to you when you asked him how your family could grow in holiness?
4. What steps can you take to help bring your family closer together?

CHAPTER 10

God can heal our beginnings

I was a child who was wanted, longed for, yearned for. The doctors had told my parents that it would be nearly impossible for them to have children. They suffered through 12 years of praying and hoping against hope that they would have a child. So there was great rejoicing when I was born. I don't know that it is possible for any child to be loved more than I was loved when I was little. My parents have a capacity for tenderness that is unique. I know that that immersion in love has been one of the reasons I search so hard for the love of God in deep prayer, in meditative prayer.

Another major reason is my grandfather, my father's father.

I called him Pop. Pop's mother, born and reared in the North
Carolina mountains, had been a full-blooded Cherokee. Pop
was steeped in an Appalachian wisdom, a Cherokee wisdom.
He never learned to read or write, yet he was one of the wisest
men I have ever known. I learned more from him about silence
and contemplation, about harmony with nature, about deep
peacefulness, than I have from the hundreds of books on theology and spirituality that I have read.

Two pictures dominated the tiny living room of my grandparents' house—the picture I have already mentioned of Jesus
standing at the door asking to be let in, and a picture of Jesus
at the Last Supper. My cousin Betty, a generation older than I,
says that Jesus was very important to Pop. He gave his heart
to Jesus in a Baptist church when he was a young man, and he
often asked Betty to read to him from the Bible.

There was a strength about Pop, a deep-down, rock-solid
strength. How comfortable he felt with silence and quiet, sitting for long periods in his chair, entering into a rich, alive stillness that showed itself in his face, his heart, his whole being.

Because I was interested in the old times, I asked Pop many
questions and delighted in his stories. His face would brighten
as I sat there on his footstool, looking at him and he at me. He
would tell me things that came from far within himself.

He would tell me marvelous stories of growing up in the
mountains of North Carolina, stories of our people that had
been handed on to him. I remember just bits and pieces of
those stories now. What I mostly remember are the feelings—
strong, powerful feelings of a different world that I was caught
up in when I listened to him. It was as though a whole new reality would spin around us as he spoke—a reality full of peace

and delight in the world, in life, in God's creatures—a reality that was at peace with a world in which God was near, not just in the Bible, but shining and reflecting himself to us through all the things around us.

I remember the first night I ever spent apart from my parents; I must have been no more than four or five years old. My father had to go to the hospital, so my mother went with him. I was restless and worried and twitched about in bed all night, crying lots of little-boy tears. When a nearby neighbor's rooster crowed, I was still awake. With the first hint of dawn, Pop got me up, helped me put on my clothes, and walked with me across the street to a path along the Chattahoochee river. We looked at Grandmother Sun as she came across the horizon above us, and then we turned and looked down at the river. We Cherokees personify nature just as Psalm 148 personified nature: "Praise him, sun and moon, praise him, all you shining stars" (Ps 148:3). We call the sun "Grandmother." We don't see Grandmother Sun as a God or Spirit but as an emblem of the one creator's love.

There was an interchange of stillness between Pop's heart and the water below and the rising sun. It was as if he were drawing on a deep quiet from creation, a quiet in which God came to us, showing his tender love through the things he made. Then Pop looked at me and gently taught me a Cherokee prayer, a prayer to Grandmother Sun. It goes like this:

> *Good morning, Grandmother Sun,*
> *Good morning, Grandmother,*
> *I stand in the middle of your sun rays,*
> *I stand in the middle of your sun rays,*
> *And by the Creator, I am blessed.*

As he said the prayer, I felt some of that stillness. Part of the pain as I grew up was that nobody else really understood the world quite like Pop. That part of me that tasted the stillness and the wonder and drank in his stories was a part no one else understood. Through Pop, I was being called to a place inside where all things are one. I had known great tenderness from my parents and aunts and uncles and such richness from Pop. But the world of school and the world of my peers laughed at Pop's way of looking at things. So I had to learn to hide that part of me.

I'm sure many of the things he shared with me were things only partially remembered from when he was little. Pop was his full-blooded Indian mother's second child. She was a "healer," a "granny woman." She had given her heart to Jesus and was baptized as a youngster. My dad said she could cure anything with herbs. And, in part because of his experiences of her, my own father developed the heart of a healer, the heart of a peacemaker.

Pop seemed always to be going back to the pantry. I used to delight in Pop's trips to that wondrously mysterious place. There were all sorts of bright and interesting things there. It seemed that almost every week he would bring me an old silver dollar from the pantry. Some had dates that went back to the 1880s. He would also show me things he said he would give me when I grew up: a mold that you poured lead into to make a bullet; an old iron, black and rusted with age, the type they used, he said, long before he was born. There were all sorts of things buried in the deep darkness of that pantry.

One day, a day I will always remember, I was sitting on his

footstool and he in his chair, when he said, "Let's go to the pan-try." I followed him with delight and expectation. I saw him pull up a board and under that board was a white beaded belt. Cherokees traditionally hold beaded belts when they have sa-cred things to say. It had yellowed and looked very old. Pop had me sit in his chair, and he sat on the stool. I didn't understand what was going on, but I wasn't afraid. He wrapped the belt around our hands clasped together, and he began to sing quiet-ly some hymns in Cherokee. I could just catch a word here and there, but it was as though powerful streams of warmth flowed from his hands through my arms and into my heart as he sang. I sat there crying—not my little-boy tears but tears such as I saw women cry when people came down to accept Christ at the invitation at the Baptist church. I saw that Pop was crying too. I had never seen Pop cry before and I never would again, nor do I know anyone else who ever saw him cry.

I didn't know what all that meant. But I knew it was sacred and special, and I knew that he was passing on to me some-thing rich and deep within him from our Cherokee people, something that had been passed to him by his full-blooded mother: a way of looking at things.

Pop became seriously ill with cancer and fought a long fight that lasted five years. He was never fully himself again. Things changed and I didn't have a chance to spend much time alone with him again. I gradually began to stuff the things he had taught me into some hidden corner within. Nobody at school talked like that or saw the world like that. None of my friends and acquaintances seemed to understand when I told them about those things. People just didn't see the world that way.

Two or three months before Pop died, my junior high school

went on half-day rotation and I spent my afternoons off with him and Granny. One day, when he looked particularly ill, he said something Indian again. As he looked at me, his eyes cleared for a moment and he smiled and said, "You walk in my soul." That was the Cherokee way of saying, "I love you." Then he said, "Remember, I used to live in Leicester, North Carolina. I want you to go there and see it someday." It was 20 years later, but one day I did.

I stuffed those things down within me. It hurt to take those memories out and look at them. I turned numb before Pop died, so very numb. I didn't cry at his funeral. I just didn't feel anything. The numbness didn't take away the pain of losing him; it just buried it deep within.

In the years after Pop's death much of my sensitivity to emotion, to life, shut down. I was a little boy, and my loss was overwhelming. I did what many children do at such a time: I walled my good memories of him from my awareness. It was many years later when I was well along the road to healing, at a time when I was strong enough and secure enough to feel the feelings of loss, that I could remember him.

Deacon Robert Herrmann and I were giving a series of retreats and evenings of renewal for the diocese of Marquette in Upper Peninsula Michigan. Our host took us to meet Father John Haskell, pastor of the Catholic Church on the small Ojibwa reservation. Father John is an Indian priest of mixed Cherokee and Ojibwa heritage involved in the cursillo movement. He was the Catholic priest to his people, richly blending Indian cultural ways with Christianity. Unity with nature; reverence for life; seeing Gitche Manitou, the Great Spirit, in all things; a communal, noncompetitive approach to life—all these gifts that came to him from his Indian heritage richly seasoned his Christianity. He viewed life as Pop had viewed it.

As I listened to Father John talk I was a bit skeptical of why anyone would bother with such quaint, irrelevant traditions. I briefly mentioned that I was part Indian. I had always known that I was Indian, and as a child I had spent time with Pop. But I tried not to think of those memories.

When I returned to Georgia I followed up on my talk with Father John. I started asking my father questions. He took me to Alabama to see Aunt Nellie, Pop's 90-year-old sister-in-law. Nellie knew so much and treasured so much.

Something was stirring inside me, something powerful at my very core. Meeting Father Haskell had lit a fuse tied to explosive emotions within me. The fuse was slowly burning shorter and shorter.

Not long after visiting with Nellie, I was recounting the conversation with Robert and Pat, my co-workers. A little while after I started talking, my eyes burned with tears and an utterly unexpected volcano of emotions burst forth from me in racking, uncontrollable sobs. Robert and Pat sat there with me, warmly present and silent as the pain erupted.

I had finally begun to grieve for Pop. I was finally strong enough to feel the loss, secure enough to at last remember. After the weeping, memories came—a few at first, then more. My grieving is still going on, but with it comes the lost joy, the lost wonder. Right along with the hurting comes the gift of my Indian heritage that Pop passed on to me. With it comes the memory of Pop's closeness to Jesus. I have experienced a flood of richness from my time of beginning as a human being—not only memories of Pop but of the wonder-filled early times with my parents, my aunts, my uncles, and the knowledge of how deeply and how thoroughly I was loved.

We all have rich resources and memories from our beginnings. We all have the bright heritage from that wondrous fresh world that once was ours. And we all have grieving to do, pain to feel, tears to shed, and people to forgive from those beginning times.

Our relationships with our parents and other close relatives go to the very heart of our own identities. We may hold inside us an unresolved resentment, anger, or deep hurt that we have never opened up for healing. Such buried anger or bitterness impairs our lives in the here and now. We also have bright, glowing memories of our parents and close relatives that are hidden away inside.

We cannot be selective in our memory. If we exile our hurtful memories, we have to hide away the joyful memories. We have to deny wonder and that whole rich symphony of feelings God made us feel. When we embrace the hurt, then the joy can flood us. When we remember the good memories, we then have the strength and sense of safety we need to face the painful ones. There are strong, wonderful, and powerful gifts from our parents and other close relatives that have gone to sleep inside us. Reawakening them can bring a springtime of fresh newness for us.

PRAYER EXPERIENCE

In this meditation, you are going to go back to the time your mother first held you in her arms. You don't need to know the actual details, but if you do know them that's helpful.

Take time to center, to be still. You may want to use one of the other meditations in this book that is particularly comforting to you. Take time to recall an occasion when your body and your heart vibrated with well-being, when health and energy, joy and happiness welled up within you, when you were surrounded by the radiant light of God's love. Remember such a time for a moment as part of your preparation for this meditation.

You are going to go back to the time of your infancy. Go back to the hospital (or home) where you were born. Your mother is in bed. She looks tired from having given birth. Perhaps she is groggy from the anesthesia. You hear steps. Someone is bringing a baby, the infant you once were. That person gently carries the baby into the room and puts it in your mother's arms. Look at your mother's facial expressions. How does she react? How does the baby respond to the mother? The adult you is in the room watching your mother with the infant. If you sense pain or distress in the room, gently pray in your own way that the healing light of Christ will fill the room to soothe and heal. If there is great rejoicing there, let yourself enter into that. As you are present there, allow the radiant love of the healing Christ to fill the inner spaces of the room.

You say a prayer for the baby and for the mother. In your own words, pray that any hidden pain will come to the surface and be healed. Now the adult you steps over to your mother. You take the baby, the infant you, from her arms. You cradle the baby. See if you can sense the needs of the infant. Pass on to the child your own deep love with the gentleness and tenderness of your touch.

Beside you comes Another. Jesus is there with you. Feel his hand on your shoulder. Feel his robe touch you. Through his touch, he passes on to you the warm compassion of his heart, the graceful and gentle power that heals. Your breathing becomes easy and slow as you are filled with a heavenly calm, and you pass that tenderness on to the infant.

DISCUSSION QUESTIONS

1. What are some of the gifts from your childhood that you carry with you today?
2. What does it mean to awaken those gifts?
3. What do you think it means to push feelings way down inside?
4. In the prayer experience what was it like to hold the infant you?

CHAPTER 11

Prayer that breaks the cycle of worry

I am an only child, and when I was growing up, my cousins were like my brothers and sisters. My cousin Billy Joe, who was eight years older than me, was my big brother in my mind. He took me on my first camping trip when I was 11. We went out into the wilderness. Night fell. We put up the tent.

Billy Joe soon fell hard and fast asleep, snoring lightly. I got in my sleeping bag and looked out the open flap of the tent in the moonlight, and what do I see, but a big black bear, shifting his weight from one leg to the other. I was too frightened to wake up Billy Joe. After all, he might make a noise and then the bear would really stampede us. I couldn't sleep a wink that night. Instead, I looked out at that bear, my eyes fixed in terror, all night long.

Then, with the coming of the first light of morning, what do I see, but a sweat shirt on a tree limb, blowing back and forth in the wind.

I have a spiritual announcement for you. Ninety percent of the bears in your life are really sweatshirts. We blow things out of proportion. We awfulize, catastrophize, as the psychotherapists put it.

Several years ago I preached a mission in a moderate-size parish in the Southwest. The attendance was high on the first night. People listened with animated faces. And yet, while the congregation seemed to enjoy the first talk, the pastor sat up front, his face stern and emotionless. Immediately I feared the worst. Surely something I said had angered him.

After I finished the talk, the pastor came up to me and said, "Tomorrow could you come by my office? I want to discuss this talk with you." Now I was certain that I had upset him and that he would call me to task. My imagination ran wild with scene after scene of possible grim outcomes. The pastor might call my diocese and tell them I did a lousy job. His assessment of my talk would pass throughout his diocese, and I would never receive an invitation to speak in that state again. Sleepless much of that night, I fought with the covers till nearly morning.

When I entered his office late the next morning, my heart

pounded. Fear gripped me. But as I sat down, I noticed this time his face was full of expression. He smiled broadly. "The talk you gave was one the best I have ever heard on the subject of prayer. I was wondering, do you have a tape of that talk? If so, could we use it in our adult education program?" As it turned out, his emotionless face the night before had simply been the result of tiredness and had nothing to do with me or the talk. My worries proved baseless, as worries often are. I had been doing what psychologists call "awfulizing" or "catastrophizing," blowing concerns out of proportion, making them far worse than they really are.

Worry—A disease of the imagination

In his book *Worry,* Harvard Medical School psychiatrist Edward M. Hallowell calls worry "a disease of the imagination." When fear and stress rise to the cerebral cortex, the mind imagines the worst possibilities. Our thoughts turn toxic, thinking of possible dire consequences. When we worry, a slide show of terrible possibilities flows through our minds. Worries come unbidden, lessening our enjoyment of work, our friends and family, and even God.

Hallowell, a practicing Christian, suggests that worry is a form of fear. When fear reaches the cerebral cortex—the part of the brain that thinks and feels, remembers and imagines— thoughts and emotion are added to the fear, deepening its power. Worry leaves us with an intense sense of powerlessness and vulnerability.

Hallowell says that when worry is at its worst, "worry can be a relentless scavenger, roaming the corners of your mind, feeding on anything, never leaving you alone." When overcome by worry, Hallowell says, "Don't wring your hands, clasp them… Prayer or meditation can change the state of your brain…Talk to God when you feel worried."

"Toxic" Worry

Some worry is good for us. A student preparing for a test needs a degree of worry to motivate good study habits. A mother with an infant should have at least some worry to remind her to watch her child closely. However, worry turns toxic when it interferes with our daily functioning, preoccupies us, or drags us down.

Hallowell says one of the early meanings of the word worry was "to gnaw." A dog digs up a bone, shakes it, grinds it, growls with it in his mouth. In short, he "worries" the bone. While worrying the bone, the dog doesn't see the beauty of the afternoon sun. He is too preoccupied. Just as the dog will not let go of the bone, a worried person won't let go of the object of his or her concern, says Hallowell, "biting and chewing it into the quick of his life. Nipping and picking and looking for meat but only finding bones and remnants."

Prayer breaks the cycle of worry

So, how can we break this cycle of "toxic" worry and begin to live a life of freedom and grace? When worries grow severely toxic, talking out your worries with a trained doctor or therapist is essential. Talking worries over with a trusted family member or friend can also help.

And yet, talking with God about our concerns is every bit as important if we truly want to gain a sense of peaceful perspective. Generations have found prayer to be a huge antidote to worry. Prayer breaks the cycle of constantly digging up our worries and chewing on them over and over again.

A prayer

Dear Lord, you made us to be close to you, near you. You have linked our heart with yours. You know how to calm us as no one else can. Your very touch can lighten our loads. It is so easy, Lord, to be overcome with worry, so easy for a problem to gnaw at us as a dog gnaws on a bone. Only your intervention can break the cycle of worry, the cycle of stress.

Today please help us to remember our worries, one by one, and to entrust each of them to you. It is so easy to worry about the past, the present, and the future. It's so easy for imaginations to run wild with thoughts of dire consequences. Come to us now, Lord Jesus; lift up our hearts and bring us your peace. Empty us of worry and fear; then fill us with your presence. Amen.

Prayer experience

You are seated in a chair. Directly in front of you is Jesus. He has come to comfort you. His presence brings a deep calm. He has come as your friend and as your savior. He knows that you are carrying many stresses and worries. And he says to you, "Let me help you with your anxiety."

As he says this, a wonderful light surrounds the two of you. It is the light of Christ omnipresent. You breathe in the light; you take it into your lungs. It warms you; it comforts you. Christ extends both arms, palms facing upward. You know what he wants you to do: he wants you to place your palms over his, so that your palms are touching. You feel the tender love of Jesus flow from his hands into yours. He wants you to allow all the stresses, tensions, and worries inside you to pass through you, out through the palms of your hands into his hands. You feel your stresses and worries just flow out of you into Jesus' palms. You feel a great experience of lightness because Jesus has been here to help you.

DISCUSSION QUESTIONS

1. What do you think the difference is between "toxic" worry and ordinary worry like the anxiety you may feel about a test?
2. How do you think prayer breaks the cycle of worry?
3. Have you ever had a worry that was like a dog gnawing at a bone, not letting go? What was it like?
4. In the prayer experience, what did it feel like having your palms meet Jesus' palms?

CHAPTER 12

Lectio Divina:

Letting Scripture transform
our emotions

Ayear after the death of her husband, Lucille was still in the grips of crisis. She and her husband had both been in their 60s when he died. For two decades they had taught the techniques of good communication within marriage to hundreds of people on retreat weekends called Marriage Encounter. Always genuinely in love with each other, their work with Marriage Encounter simply deepened their bonds and their love for one another. Countless times they gave talks about how good communication and spirituality helped keep marriages close.

That made her husband's death particularly tragic for Lucille.

She had never thought or planned to live alone. Prayer was especially difficult. They had always taken their quiet times together, and she was not use to praying alone. She carried a weight of grief and stress. Lucille had read about *lectio divina* (divine reading) in a magazine, and she decided to try it. She picked a passage from Isaiah 40, and slowly began reading to herself, savoring each word.

"Comfort, my people, says your God.
Speak tenderly to Jerusalem and cry to her
that her warfare is ended."

Lucille read over the passage two or three times slowly before something truly touched her: "Speak tenderly to Jerusalem." Delicately she began repeating the phrase. Gradually she felt led to shorten it, praying, "Speak tenderly...speak tenderly...speak tenderly."

A gentle love quietly welled up within her. She rested for a moment in the silence of that love. "Speak tenderly to me, Oh Lord. Speak tenderly to me." She slowly repeated that prayer until her heart quieted. She then rested in the silence for five or ten minutes. Later, she said to me, "Praying that Scripture helped me to feel, for the first time since my husband died, that God loved me tenderly." As she daily prayed this way, an abiding sense of God's presence filled her heart. Of course, *lectio divina* did not take away the pain from the loss of her husband, but it did give her a sense that when she prayed, she was not alone. "I know I will always grieve for him until my own death," she said to me. "But I know for sure now that there is indeed someone who holds me close beside my husband, God. And I can converse with him at any moment and I can hear God converse with me, through Scripture."

Getting to the heart of Scripture

If we are to draw close to the heart of God, we must be willing to listen for his still, small voice (1 Kgs 19:9–18). "They are the faint, murmuring sounds…[of] God's word for us, God's voice touching our hearts," observes Luke Dysinger, O.S.B., who describes *lectio divina* as "accepting the embrace of God." Often we want to read the Scriptures to obtain knowledge and meaning. We can never do without Bible study; the Bible is divine revelation, after all. For Bible study we need to read Scripture in context and often consult good commentaries.

Lectio divina is a different way of reading—a more intimate reading of Scripture, a reading with the heart. *Lectio divina* is also a way of prayerful listening for the soft, quiet voice of God. Saint Benedict called *lectio divina* listening "with the ear of our hearts."

So, how does one begin? There are four simple steps.

1. Begin with prayer.

Before you actually begin, take time to grow quiet in prayer, perhaps by using the Jesus Prayer. Take deep breaths and allow your heart to settle into a deep calm.

2. "Tolle, lege": Take up and read.

Next is the *lectio* or reading. Pick a passage of Scripture to read slowly. You may want to read it several times, each time a little more slowly and with longer pauses between lines and phrases, enabling the meaning to sink deep into the soul. Usually most people read each passage at least two times. Consciously slow your reading. The speed with which we read newspapers or articles on the Web is not appropriate for *lectio divina*. One of the best ways to slow yourself down is to quietly read the passage aloud. Some people feel uncomfortable reading aloud, but give it a try. If you still feel uncomfortable reading aloud, just repeat the words slightly under your breath. Move your tongue but enunciate the words just under your breath. Read it slowly. Savor it. Let the feelings of the Scripture get inside you.

3. Ponder, ruminate, and meditate.

Finally, we move to *meditatio* or meditation. When a phrase resonates within us as we are reading, we "ruminate" on it, just like an animal chews its cud. We ponder it with the heart. When you come to such a word or phrase, repeat it slowly several times. After you have savored and repeated the word or phrase, rest in stillness a moment, as long as it seems right to you. This rest is a wordless basking in the presence of the one who loves us without measure. Your heart will instinctively apply the word or phrase to your life. When you come to a phrase or word that touches you, repeat it over and over again very slowly. It will take on a kind of anointing. For instance, if you are reading Psalm 23—"The Lord is My Shepherd, I shall not want, he makes me to lie down in green pastures…he restores my soul"—the phrase "restores my soul" may seem particularly significant, something to savor. Just repeat that over and over, as long as the grace of the moment lasts.

4. Deepen your contemplation.

When you are ready, close your Bible and close your eyes. It is the time for intimate conversation with God: verbal prayer. A phrase or a word may so inspire you that you offer a prayer to

God, and then perhaps hear his wordless, "still, small voice." Don't worry about having the "right" words to offer God. It is in the silence that we allow God to do what he wants to do most of all, simply love us. This is a wordless prayer, a resting, a stillness.

Such prayer is a gift of God, an invitation to intimate union. Anyone who has been in love knows that there are moments of wordless communion when hearts seem as one. This may seem complicated, but it really isn't. The parts of *lectio divina* don't necessarily come in exact set stages. For instance, you might feel an inspiration to offer a prayer early in the reading. If you do, stop and pray. You may feel yourself drawn to repeat a word or phrase and ruminate over it. Do so at any time. You may be drawn in to the loving stillness of contemplation at any moment. If you do, stop and rest silently in God's presence. You will know when it is time to begin reading the passage again.

A PRAYERFUL READING (*LECTIO DIVINA*)

Read this passage slowly, frequently pausing to listen for the still, small voice of God.

"Do not let your hearts be troubled. Believe in God, believe also in me. In my Father's house there are many dwelling places. If it were not so, would I have told you that I go to prepare a place for you? And if I go and prepare a place for you, I will come again and will take you to myself, so that where I am, there you may be also...Peace I leave with you; my peace I give to you. I do not give to you as the world gives. Do not let your hearts be troubled, and do not let them be afraid" (John 14:1-3, 27).

CHAPTER 13

How wonder heals

Mark was a person whose plans seemed always to succeed. A superb athlete in high school, he helped carry his team to the state finals in basketball. He was a straight-A student and yet he was popular at the same time. He came from one of those homes that seemed to be free of major problems. His parents always let their children express their feelings and opinions. Mark exuded healthiness.

A bout with hepatitis that nearly took his life when he was 14 somehow deepened him. He could talk with bright eyes about the latest music and loved to go to dances, yet he always took time each night to read the Bible and say a short prayer.

When I met Mark, he was a senior in college. He told me that his life had begun to seem dry. Something was missing. Although his degree in engineering and his excellent record in college would guarantee him a high-paying job, he had been struggling for months with a decision to spend two years in Latin America as a lay volunteer. He attended one of our twilight retreats and talked to me afterward. He said that the whole idea of meditative and contemplative prayer seemed to open new horizons for him.

Mark was a person who loved to get into things and do them well and thoroughly. He began to do something that is very rare in healthy young people: he started taking an hour a day for prayer. He would stop by the campus church after his last class and spend an hour there every day.

One night several weeks later, while he was studying, a deep sense of resting in God's love came over him—a sense of being cradled in a tingling, vibrant love that warmed him to the very core of his being. Warm currents flowed through his body, and a deep stillness settled in. In the gentlest of transitions, a beautiful light filled the room; a dazzling light surrounded him. Mute with wonder, he was totally immersed in brightness, warmth, and peace, bathed in emotions of joy, rapture, and reverential awe. It was as though senses new within him awakened. It was a timeless moment. His eyes brimmed with tears. He stayed there in the midst of the light for 20 or 30 minutes, weeping because of the peace that came over him. The light gradually faded, but he sat there most of the night, awake, resting in peacefulness.

In the following weeks, Mark kept up his hour of prayer

and said a strong yes to the two years of missionary work. He wanted to give to others some of the goodness that had been given to him.

Experiences such as Mark's are far more common than we realize. You cannot will such an experience; you cannot choose when such a timeless moment comes. It comes as a gracious gift, and it comes with God's timing.

Mark was wise, too, not to make more of the experience than warranted. He knew that it is the steady encounter of God in our daily lives that counts. Although experiences such as Mark's can widen us, give us hope, and nudge us on a bit, I don't think it is wise to seek after them in their own right.

Such religious experiences are usually a by-product of our everyday experience of God. There is always a strong human element in such graced times. Our unconscious plays a very clear role. This side of glory no one has a "direct line." Revelation ended with Jesus Christ. Yet, of course, God can be very much in such wondrous times, as he is in all aspects of our living and feeling. We seek the experience of God, not the God of experiences.

Marriage helps illustrate this. Giddy feelings of falling in love can come to a couple many times during their marriage, or during their courtship. The feelings of being close come when couples genuinely share their feelings, forgiving one another and acknowledging their anger if they need to.

So it is with God. We don't look for the feeling of closeness by itself. What we seek are lives that are informed by the gospel, changed by the gospel to move in the right direction. We talk about such powerful religious experiences because they are part of the landscape. We should neither repress them nor give them undue importance.

God's love transcends our logical knowledge. When we open ourselves to him, we open ourselves to the dimension of the wondrous, to the spiritual world, to an experience beyond words. When I think of wonder, I think of children two to five years old. The sense of life's mystery has not been bleached out of them. They take a leaf, hold it in their hands, and delight in it; they grab a spring flower and giggle with joy. Just watching a train go by becomes an adventure. Society educates much of the sense of wonder out of us, but when we open ourselves to God's love, to prayer, wonder is reborn in us.

In his moving novel *Creek Mary's Blood,* Dee Brown tells the story of a Cherokee Indian who entered into the wonder of the spiritual world. The book is the *Gone with the Wind* of the American Indians. Part of the story involves a well-educated Cherokee named Dane who acted as a scout for wagon trains moving west. Later he married a Cheyenne and joined the Cheyenne tribe. The Cheyenne religion, like much North American Indian spirituality, resembles Christian spirituality.

An important event in Dane's life was his entry into what he called "the real world." By this he meant the spiritual world, the dimension of the wondrous. Describing his spiritual discovery to a reporter, Dane said:

> *I lived with the Cheyenne a long time before I learned how to cross into the real world, and all that time my wife and children could do this and they were puzzled because I could not join them there....I was finally able to find my way into the real world with my family. I discovered mysterious powers within my memory and learned that when you pray for others to become strong you become strong, too, because that connects*

you with everything else. You become a part of every-
thing and that is how I knew that I was necessary to
my family and they were necessary to me…."What is it
like, the real world?" the reporter asked.

He remained silent for a while and then spoke slowly.

"Being a man who loves words, I have often thought about that. But some things cannot be put into words. The closest I ever came was an English word. Shimmering."

"Shimmering?"

"Yes, like swimming in moonlight."

Not only does wonder put us in touch with God; it can become a channel of his healing us individually and together.

In 1979 I was speaking at a meeting in Mexico City. This visit came just after speaking at a conference at the Anaheim convention center in California and spending a week giving retreats in the Archdiocese of Los Angeles. I was at the very beginning of my ministry of giving talks and retreats. I felt overwhelmed by the responsibility. The success of my first book, *Sounds of Wonder,* had resulted in a large number of speaking engagements, and standing up and attempting to speak gave me butterflies in the very core of my being. I was haunted by memories of when I was a child, failing at many things because of a learning disability brought on by right hemisphere brain dysfunction, likely from a birth injury.

Under the pressure of my schedule, old wounds began to hurt again. I particularly worried about the talk I was to give to a Mexican leadership conference at San José Altillo, near the University of Mexico.

Before the conference, in my free time, I thought it would be interesting, maybe even inspiring, to see the sacred cloth that contained the image of Mary as Our Lady of Guadalupe.

It ended up being a pilgrimage that forever touched my life. I saw tens of thousands of people, many with tattered clothes that indicated their poverty and their need, praying with deep emotion in the huge square that led to the Basilica. Most of them were on their knees inching forward, saying and chanting prayers as tears rolled down their faces. Powerful waves of God's presence swept through all of us. These people believed, not just in their minds but in their hearts and their entire body. Never have I seen such a depth of belief in one place.

Wonder overcame me and swept away my hurts.

Wonder can seep away hurts for all of us. We have our insecurities, our long-ago wounds. A dose of God's magnificence, a taste of wonder, drives away those hurts.

Scripture Journey

We are going to enter a scene from the Bible you have probably read about many times: the scene from the sixth chapter of Isaiah, which records Isaiah's vision in the temple when he saw the Lord in all his majesty and glory.

> *In the year that King Uzziah died I saw the Lord sitting upon a throne, high and lifted up; and his train filled the temple. Above him stood the seraphim; each had six wings: with two, he covered his face, and with two he covered his feet, and with two he flew. And one called to another and said: "Holy, holy, holy is the Lord of hosts; and the whole earth is full of his glory."*
>
> *And the foundations of the thresholds shook at the voice of him who called, and the house was filled*

with smoke. And I said; "Woe is me! For I am lost; for
I am a man of unclean lips, and I dwell in the midst of
a people of unclean lips; for my eyes have seen the
King, the Lord of hosts!"
Then flew one of the seraphim to me, having in his
hand a burning coal which he had taken with tongs
from the altar. And he touched my mouth and said,
"Behold, this has touched your lips; your guilt is taken
away, and your sin forgiven." And I heard the voice of
the Lord saying, "Whom shall I send, and who will go
for us?" Then I said, "Here am I! Send me." (Is 6:1–8)

The time is not now; the time is that period in ancient Israel.
It's a glorious day and the sun shines brightly. You are standing outside the temple—a huge churchlike building. A man
dressed in robes comes out of the temple. His facial muscles
are at ease, loose and relaxed, emanating a radiant glow. His
eyes sparkle brightly, full of wonder and mystery. This is Isaiah,
and he has just emerged from an overwhelming experience of
the Lord—the experience you have just read about.

Isaiah looks at you and says simply, "Now it is your turn."

You slowly enter the temple. There is no need to picture ex-
actly what the temple is like; just go in and find a comfortable
seat.

Perhaps you feel some fear, some puzzlement. You sense
you will encounter the same majestic presence, the same overwhelming vision that Isaiah has just experienced. You know
that such an experience can awaken abilities and gifts that are
buried inside you—abilities to sense and feel that you have
never used before. Wherever the Lord is, wherever God's love

is, there is also ease and peace and warmth and tender kindness for those who open their hearts to him.

Close your eyes. The scene that is about to unfold is not one that you can picture fully with your conscious mind. Just having a vague sense of that scene taking place before you is enough. Your eyes are closed now, and after a moment you become aware that the Lord is in the temple, sitting on his throne, high and lifted up. The train of his robe fills the temple. Above him stand the seraphim. One calls out, "Holy, holy, holy is the Lord of hosts; the whole earth is full of his glory."

You bask in a tender awe, a hushed wonder. Let the wonder and awe begin to sink into you, flowing through your skin into your deepest self. There is no need to intensify or try to feel the feelings; just have a sense of the feelings inherent in such a scene, a vague sense that these feelings of wonder and awe are like a cloud or other airy substance sinking into your depths. The feelings will come at the time that's right for you. Perhaps later as you go about your daily life, your unconscious may release powerful images that help you taste and drink in the scene.

You hear the loud call of the seraph reverberating in the temple: "Holy, holy, holy is the Lord of hosts; the whole earth is full of his glory." You can feel the vibrations of the loud voice going up through your legs, through all of you. Perhaps like Isaiah, you feel a great sense of unworthiness and fear to be in the midst of such a scene. Do you? What are some things in your daily life that make you fearful? Just become aware of those feelings; there is no need to judge.

One of the seraphim puts a hot coal in your mouth. You feel the coal in your mouth. Instead of a searing, burning pain, you feel a warmth that surprises you. The gentle and firm warmth from the coal spreads down through your throat, cleansing you. It flows farther down, into your heart, expanding into a ball of glowing, warming light within your heart. It goes down your spine, warming, cleansing, and healing. Reaching the base of your spine, it brings the tingling warmth there, too. You feel purified all over by the burning coal.

The Lord says to you, "Whom shall I send? And who will go?" See if you, like Isaiah, are able to say yes to that request. If you are, move your lips and say, "I will go, Lord. Send me." In doing this meditation, do not struggle to feel any particular feelings. The meditation is designed to prime and open up your heart so that your unconscious can pour forth feelings and insights later. During the actual meditation, you may feel dry. Yet the next day or the next week, you may find yourself tasting a fiery awe in everyday life, feeling the wonder of God, experiencing a new humility, a new purity, a new cleansing.

DISCUSSION QUESTIONS

1. Can you think of a time wonder has touched you? If so tell about it.
2. What do you think the phrase "God transcends our logical knowledge" means?
3. In the prayer experience, what did it feel like for the angel to put the coal on your lips?
4. Can you think of times when an experience of God prompted someone to get personally involved in the work of God's Kingdom? If so, tell about it.

CHAPTER 14

Healing our world

I well remember the last vacation I took with my father. It was in 1995. Mother and Aunt Margaret were with us too. We went up into the North Carolina Mountains. Now 84, Dad had been declining We were all tight with worry, and we feared this would be the last vacation he ever took. Dad, like my grandfather Pop, had been proud of his American Indian heritage and despite a limp, he walked through the museum at the Cherokee reservation like a young man experiencing home after a long deployment. His eyes grew moist. Memories of his upbringing returned, and he talked about them in hushed tones.

Then we drove deeper into the mountains to Leicester and Sandy Mush, where his father, Pop, was born and reared. Stories that Pop had told him and stories Pop had told me came to our lips as we both quietly talked together on the edge of the whirling whitewater over stone, the French Broad River.

The sound of rustling water penetrated both our hearts. The clouds against a blue sky and the encircling mountains spoke one word to both of us. It was evident from the sacred stillness that grasped us what that word was—God. God had guided our family's history. He made the beauty of the scene that surrounded us. The mountains, the sky, the rushing water, and the wind that beat down on us were his vestments.

The same scenes that had enriched the soul of my grandfather now enriched Dad and me.

Later, when Dad died several months afterward, I said a prayer of thanks for the time we had a chance to spend by the French Broad River.

Scenes and sounds from nature are bright threads woven throughout the cloth of Scripture. It seems as though the biblical writers cannot speak of God without using images and comparisons from nature. "I will lift up my eyes to the hills, from whence comes my help. My help comes from the Lord" (Ps 121:1). "As the mountains are round about Jerusalem, so the Lord is round about his people" (Ps 125:2). "Bless the Lord, O my soul! O Lord my God, you are very great! You are clothed with honor and majesty." You "cover yourself with light as with a garment." You "make the clouds your chariot" and "ride on the wings of the wind." You "make the winds your messengers, fire and flame your ministers." You "make springs gush forth in the valleys; they flow between the hills" (Ps 104:1–10).

As the sensitive, God-filled poet Gerard Manley Hopkins tells us: "The world is charged with the grandeur of God. It will flame out, like shining from shook foil; it gathers to a greatness, like the ooze of oil...Because the Holy Ghost over the bent world broods with warm breast and with ah! bright wings."

When Jesus prayed, he went out to be with nature. Whenever he needed refreshment, whenever he needed healing, whenever he needed deep communion with the Father, he went away to the hills and the water. Much of God's healing comes through his creation around us. Jesus knew that. Such phrases as "Look at the birds in the sky, the lilies of the field" fill his speech. All his imagery shows a profound communion with creation. The two main characteristics of Jesus' prayer were his *abba* experience of the love of the Father and his communion with creation all around him. That sensitivity to nature shows itself in his style of speaking.

Saint Bonaventure wrote, "In creation we see the footprints of God." Nature can be a source, a channel for God's presence coming to us. Remembering nature expands our capacity for experiencing God every day in his creation.

Yet despite the beautiful scenes in nature that so bind us to God, our earth, our environment is wounded by the avarice and addictions of people. Not all scenes are as pristine as the North Carolina Mountains. I think the phrase some people use—"our earth is being raped by its people"—is not too strong.

We can easily miss our interconnectedness with all creation. A brilliant Navajo student and faithful Catholic left the reservation to attend university but after three years decided to leave and return to the reservation. His friends were upset, saying, "You have thrown away your future. You have so much promise. Why?"

The young Navajo answered their questions by drawing two circles. In one he drew a large person in its center. In the other circle he drew several persons, several animals, trees, a hill. He looked to the circle that had only a man in the center and said, "This is the modern civilized world of the university and society."

Then he pointed to the picture of man, nature, and animals together, and said: "This is God's world."

Our earth is a wounded earth. Our massive attempts to conquer the earth have scarred creation. As Saint Paul says, together with all creation, we groan for redemption. (See Rom 8:22–23.) Only when we acknowledge that we are part of the net that binds together all God's creation does real healing flow into our being.

The U.S. bishops' pastoral letter *Renewing the Earth* puts it this way, "Humanity's arrogance and acquisitiveness, however, led time and again to our growing alienation from nature" (see Gn 3—4, 6—9, 11ff).

Blessed Pope John Paul II has called for Christians to respect and protect the environment, so that through nature people can "contemplate the mystery of the greatness and love of God."

Eastern Church father Isaac of Nineveh says that the experience of God opens us up to our connection with all creatures: "The heart that is inflamed in this way embraces the entire creation—man, birds, animals At the recollection of them, and at the sight of them, such a man's eyes fill with tears that arise from the great compassion which presses on his heart."

Since 1995 most scientists have agreed that today's warming of the earth is brought about mainly by fossil fuels.

Just small rises in temperature impact the earth: more heat waves, more drought, and more drastic weather events such as floods, more tropical disease, and fiercer hurricanes.

The poor, by far, are those whom climate change hits hardest. For no other reason than that it affects "the least of these" so severely, Christians should work to change policy and law to lower fossil emissions. John Taylor, advocacy officer for Catholic Relief Services, already sees the impact of environmental change on the poor. In 1970, he says, 65 natural disasters were recorded. Three hundred and eighty-eight were recorded in 2007. Around the world people depend on agriculture just to survive. Those are the ones most impacted.

Christian Aid, a British relief organization, calculates that by 2050 climate change will make a billion people homeless, primarily the poor.

Renewing the Earth calls renewing the earth a "moral issue." In its moving closing the pastoral letter reaches for our hearts: "Christian love draws us to serve the weak and vulnerable among us. We are called to feed the hungry, to give drink to the thirsty, to clothe the naked, to shelter the homeless. We are also summoned to restore the land; to provide clean, safe water to drink and unpolluted air to breathe."

What we can do

The most important thing we can do is pray for our wounded earth daily; pray for its healing, its restoration. This helps us feel our connection with God and his creation as well. Use meditations like the one ending this chapter. Over time, by praying you will develop a deep compassion for all created things and those most harmed by the earth's wounds.

Do something

No one of us can solve the whole problem of climate change but we can each do something. We can recycle. We can advocate for less dependence on fossil fuels. We can drive energy efficient cars and make our houses efficient. If Christians begin to feel their connection to the earth, action will necessarily flow out of that connection.

PRAYER EXPERIENCE

When you are relaxed, prayerful, and in the loving presence of God, begin to imagine some of the beautiful scenes of nature you have seen: sunrises, sunsets, the hot beating sun coming down on you in summertime, the sound and sight of waves crashing against the sand, the sky at night, the smell of raindrops on a dusty sidewalk, the fresh air of high mountains, the beauty of mountains against the sky—special times in nature. Relive such times in your imagination—taste, sights, scents, sounds. Feel the emotions again.

Remember a nature spot that is special to you. Go there in your imagination. Sit down. Relax there for a while and allow that scene to express God's love to you.

Jesus now comes and sits beside you and puts his arm around you. The brilliant light of heaven pours forth from his heart. That light now surrounds you. Then that light begins to cascade out of your heart too. The lights all join together and begin to flood the scenes of nature laid out before you. The light flows to places where the earth has been scarred by mining, making whole again each scene. The light flows out over the entire earth, causing floods to recede when needed, rain to fall when needed. Beautifully and slowly our wounded earth is

renewed. Jesus now speaks to you. He says, "Pray each day for
the renewing of the earth. Walk with sensitivity to the land, to
the ground beneath your feet. Be aware of the goodness of the
earth and take whatever steps you can to renew it."

Discussion questions

1. What scene did your mind take you to?
2. Did you find imagining the nature calmed and stilled
   you?
3. Do you think daily taking time to imagine scenes from
   God's creation might be something you might want to
   try in your prayer?
4. What thoughts ran through your mind as you joined
   with Jesus in letting healing light pour out over the earth
   to mend and renew it?

PARISH MISSIONS, RETREATS AND CONFERENCES

The author of this book, Deacon Eddie Ensley, PhD, along with Deacon Robert Herrmann, offers parish missions, retreats, and conferences throughout the country. A parish mission by the two deacons draws the whole parish together. It recharges the congregation. Everyone takes time for the truly important things like wonder, mystery, healing, and prayer. People are reconciled. Faith is awakened. Vocations are discovered.

The deacons can also lead clergy retreats and conferences as well as religious education conferences.

To bring them to your parish or your event or to ask for an information packet about what their retreats and conferences can offer your area, you can contact them at 706-322-8840, visit their website **www.parishmission.net**, or email Deacon Ensley at **pmissions@charter.net**.

"The Mission proved to be a tremendous help for our families...Our attendance was better than ever. The guided meditations throughout were vivid and also uplifting. The parish mission was filled with solid content. The greatest compliment has been in the attendance."

FATHER JOHN T. EUKER,
St. John the Baptist, Perryopolis, Pennsylvania

Other books by Eddie Ensley

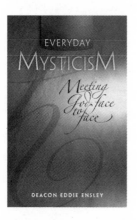

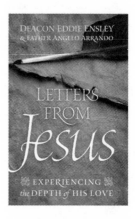

Everyday Mysticism
Meeting God Face to Face
DEACON EDDIE ENSLEY

Deacon Eddie Ensley shows us that mysticism isn't just for monastics and contemplatives. It's for each of us, every day of our lives, every time we open our hearts to God. Mysticism, he says, is a simple and profound treasure, available to us all. Inspiring and insightful for spiritual reading.

136 PAGES | $12.95
9781585958436

Letters from Jesus
Experiencing the Depth of His Love
DEACON EDDIE ENSLEY
AND FATHER ANGELO ARRANDO

Deacon Ensley and Father Arrando speak here through intimate letters from Jesus to help readers hear God speaking deep within them and thus to experience God, Jesus, and life itself as never before.

104 PAGES | $10.95
9781585958337

1-800-321-0411
www.23rdpublications.com

TWENTY
THIRD 23rd
PUBLICATIONS